THE COVID CHRONICLES

ONCE UPON A TIME, AS FASCISM, CONTAGION, AND MASS LUNACY FESTERED

W. E. GUTMAN

CCB Publishing
British Columbia, Canada

The COVID Chronicles: Once Upon A Time,
As Fascism, Contagion, and Mass Lunacy Festered

Non-fiction. Essays. History. Current events.

Copyright ©2022 by W. E. Gutman
ISBN-13   978-1-77143-549-9
First Edition

Library and Archives Canada Cataloguing in Publication
Title: The COVID chronicles : once upon a time, as fascism, contagion,
and mass lunacy festered / W.E. Gutman.
Names: Gutman, W. E., 1937- author.
Description: First edition.
Issued in print and electronic formats.
Identifiers: ISBN 978-1-77143-549-9 (pbk.).--ISBN 978-1-77143-550-5 (pdf)
Additional cataloguing data available from Library and Archives Canada

Cover design by the author.
Cover artwork courtesy of Pixabay.

This book is printed on acid-free paper.

Disclaimer by author: References to real persons, alive or dead, are contextual and crucial to the narrative. Some names have been changed to protect the identity of certain individuals.

Fair Use Notice: This work contains minor excerpts, with attribution, the use of which has not always been specifically authorized by the copyright owner. It is believed this constitutes a "fair use" of any such copyrighted material, as provided for in Section 107 of the US Copyright Law.

Extreme care has been taken by the author to ensure that all information presented in this book is accurate and up to date at the time of publishing. The publisher cannot be held responsible for any errors or omissions. Additionally, neither is any liability assumed by the publisher for damages resulting from the use of the information contained herein.

Publisher: CCB Publishing
              British Columbia, Canada
              www.ccbpublishing.com

Books by W. E. Gutman

JOURNEY TO XIBALBA:
The Subversion of Human Rights in Central America

NOCTURNES: Tales from the Dreamtime

FLIGHT FROM EIN SOF

THE INVENTOR

ONE NIGHT IN COPÁN

A PALER SHADE OF RED: Memoirs of a Radical

ONE LAST DREAM

UN DERNIER RÊVE

ALL ABOUT EARTHLINGS:
The Irreverent Musings of an Extraterrestrial Envoy

MORPHEUS POSSESSED:
The Conflict Between Dream and Reality

MORPHEUS UNCHAINED:
Remembrances of a Future Dream

MORPHEUS' CHALLENGE: Beyond the Dreams

JEU DE RÔLE : Souvenances d'un Baladin

MIRED: LIFE IN THE SWAMP: Ruminations of the Irrelevance of
Truth In an Age of Unreason, Lies, and Killer Pandemics

LES DIABLERIES DE MORPHÉE: Confessions d'un Rêveur

"You don't have to teach people how to be human.
You have to teach them how to stop being inhuman."
— **Eldridge Cleaver (1935-1998)**

"The most violent element in society is ignorance."
—Emma Goldman (1869–1940)

"What was is what will be, and what has been done
is what will be done; there is nothing
new under the sun" — (Ecclesiastes 1:9)

TO THE READER—This is an open-ended narrative. The last chapter is yet to be inferred. Nothing is set in stone. By the time you turn the last page, my assumptions, revelations, and fomentations might be in vain, and the warnings they imply too late to be heeded. Call this an epitaph before the fact. What is indisputable is that history repeats itself and that the best laid plans of mice and men often lead to decadence, chaos, and ruin. Yes, as time shrinks, as the Earth sizzles, a dwindling number among us are fated to survive so that, after an interlude of spurious contrition, melodramatic *mea culpas,* and pledges to expiate our sins, we may once again feign puritanism, wallow in debauchery, defile nature, succumb to greed, give in to anger, and make war. The present is grim. The future, divined from a witch's cauldron of toxic concoctions, is bleak.

◆

Predictable but not imminent when I began writing this book, Russia's invasion of Ukraine was a distant scenario. The horrors that would unfold, the scenes of devastation and human martyrdom copiously splattered on television were unimagined, beyond comprehension. Yet it wasn't the first time, be it cowardice or subterfuge, sham *"neutrality"* or artifice, that the sheep are led to slaughter to shield those who might come to harm by defying the wolf.

Sanctions, arms shipments, and impassioned pledges of support notwithstanding—all of which are prolonging the conflict, not ending it—Ukraine is being immolated to spare those whose moral obligation is not only to protest loudly but to intervene decisively. But that has always been and will always remain the fate, in some cases the cold-blooded stratagem, that causes entire civilizations to collapse. What we are witnessing on this side of the Atlantic, as *"Charismatic"* Christians praise *"God"* for calling upon Vladimir Putin to invade Ukraine as a prelude to Armageddon and the Second Coming, is the piecemeal obliteration of a sovereign state and the methodical slaughter of thousands of its citizens.

And while these barbarities unfold and the world looks on in disbelief and horror, some of us wonder whether the wrong word, a misperceived facial expression, or a fatal miscalculation might put an end to the hostilities—and civilization as we know it. After all, didn't Russian broadcast journalist, Margarita Simonyan, assure her audience that a nuclear war would be *"O.K. because, in any case, we're all going to die someday"* … while Russian Foreign Minister Sergey Lavrov insisted that Hitler was a Jew, and that Jews are *"the worst anti-Semites"*? Mr. Lavrov would have the world believe that the Jews had secretly plotted the *"Final Solution"* and proceeded to exterminate themselves. Likewise, Ukrainians are killing each other, shelling, and obliterating their own cities, murdering their own people, whereas Russia intervened to protect the citizens of Ukraine from Ukrainians. In 2008 Georgians were wiping each other off so Russia had to annex part of their territory to protect Georgians from Georgians. It is amazing how nations are destroying themselves and only Russia is there to save them from themselves. This enormity from a nation that warned that if NATO keeps supporting Ukraine … there will be a *"massive nuclear strike"* that will see only "mutants" survive. As Joseph Goebbels, Hitler's Propaganda Minister famously asserted, *"The greater the lie the more likely people will believe it."* This axiom, and the evil it telegraphs, would not be lost on one Donald John Trump and an assortment of Republican politicians and deranged copycats.

The urge to self-destruct by wiping out others is a powerful instinct that lays dormant when our existence is not threatened by catastrophic events. The threat of a nuclear strike by Russia, hinted at by Putin in 2018 *"if Russia is attacked,"* and echoed more ominously in late April 2022, cannot be ignored. Russia's territorial ambitions may not have ended with the conquest of Ukraine. U.S. intelligence officials have warned that, as the war grinds on over the coming months, Russia's offensive could expand, grow more volatile and bloodier, and that the use of even a tactical nuclear bomblet would be met with a massive thermonuclear response.

Meanwhile, Putin, a vile, heartless, scoundrel, seeks to erase any historical memory of Stalinist state terrorism as a means of perpetuating its impact and influence. One of Russia's most painful problems is that of historical amnesia. It is a country in a state of permanent post-traumatic stress disorder. Its most serious psychological trauma is not Germany's ill-fated 1941 offensive but the memory of Stalinist terror and the end of the world as its people knew it.

Another frightening aspect of this obscene conflict is the perplexing support of Russia's aims by many U.S. Republican politicians, most of them functionally illiterate and intellectually sterile agitators whose racist rants appeal to the lowest echelons of America's electorate. Triggered when Obama was elected and reelected, this uninhibited slide to the extreme political right is in full swing in the nation that now has the highest rate of anti-Semitic assaults and vandalism. I have always held that a Kristallnacht can happen again, even in the most *"unlikely place of all,"* as German Jews believed their country to be before Nazis, on that fateful night, torched synagogues, vandalized Jewish homes, schools, and businesses, and killed close to 100 Jews—even in America where social networks are playing an exceptionally alarming role in inspiring anti-Semitic incidents and spreading lies. There has been a 30 percent increase in anti-

3

Semitic assaults in the U.S. since last year (2021), with 416 incidents in New York, including a record 51 attacks and another 370 incidents in New Jersey.

Of course, the world as we knew it ended several times before our common era and survivors, after a brief period of fake repentance, proceeded to ravage the world all over again until the first signs of yet another impending day of reckoning loomed large on humanity's horizon. Will our reincarnated doppelgangers of, say, the 31st century, be pondering the next Götterdämmerung? The final "end," we are told, will come when the Sun dies in a final blaze of glory. As it expands, the Earth will get so hot that the oceans will boil and evaporate into space. The planet will become a burning husk that gets pulled to the sun's surface and vaporizes. By then, the world will have spawned a few prodigies and a huge number of imbeciles and villains. All attempts to establish sustainable extraterrestrial human settlements having failed, those of us who did not succumb to greed, hatred, or terminal stupidity, will marvel at the grand spectacle of a final twilight while the faithful join to seek help from an entity that has remained consistently blind, deaf, and indifferent to human suffering.

And then there's the pandemic. The resurgence (or is it the survivability in all its incarnations) of the coronavirus, adds to the proliferating hazards that threaten our existence. No one can account for its genesis. No one knows for sure what spontaneous confluence of natural phenomena (or contrived manipulations) aroused and animated it, and what unexpected miscegenation will increase its lethality. And certainly not a single infectious disease expert can predict how it will evolve and how long it will endure. As nature decays under human mismanagement, other pandemics, some far more lethal than the Covid variety can be anticipated.

The predicted sixth mass environmental extinction, an event

in which a significant portion of the world's biodiversity is forever lost, is not some distant, future event. It's happening now, much faster than previously expected and, according to a study published in the scientific journal, *Proceedings of the National Academy of Sciences*, it's entirely our fault. Humans have already obliterated hundreds of species and pushed many more to the brink through wildlife trade, deforestation, pollution, habitat loss, and the use of toxic substances. Due to global warming [the bulk of the world's scientific community agrees that the Earth is heating up and that one of the main factors of global warming is human activity] the rate at which species are dying out has accelerated exponentially in recent years. Governments must tell the truth by declaring a climate and ecological emergency. To avoid tipping points in the climate system, biodiversity loss, and the risk of social collapse, they must work to reduce greenhouse gas emissions to net-zero by 2025. Nor is an ocean mass extinction event that far off. Ocean life could die within decades at levels that rival the biggest mass extinctions in history. Yes, after decades of doing our level best to destroy the planet we inhabit, we're finally on the verge of success.

◆

Born in Crimea, an alumnus of the KGB's Military Institute of Foreign Languages (he speaks six languages), and a fierce opponent of Putin and Russian aggression in Ukraine, my old friend "Yevgeny" recently asked me: "Do humans have value?" An incurable globe-trotter and frustrated reformer now marking time somewhere in the Balkans after lengthy stints in France, the U.S., Hungary, and Turkey, he resents indifference. Neutrality infuriates him. He never misses an opportunity to point out that humans are too stupid to survive and insists that our *"unfettered mating habits"* endanger the planet. *"Nothing prevents good science from being ignored like idiocy, malice, and conspiratorial silence,"* he asserts. He is willing to bet his last kopek that no one will ever lift a finger to save the world from itself, not even when it sinks into an irreversible coma. He calls humans *"talkative apes"* and finds *"mankind's obsession with longevity"* repulsive. His nihilism is refreshing.

"Do humans have value?" The question startled me as it was uttered with almost childlike candor, not with "Yevgeny's" characteristic sarcasm. Rhetorical questions merit prosaic rejoinders. I replied:

> *"Yes, but only at the most intimate level. We cherish our parents, children, siblings, friends, colleagues. We also revere creative geniuses (great philosophers, writers, poets, composers, painters, sculptors, etc.). We place less worth on the perfect strangers who cross our paths in our daily meanderings, and far less yet on that faceless, amorphous multitude called 'humankind,' that nebulous mass we pity in passing while thinking of something else."*

Those who claim to profess an unconditional *"love"* for humankind, I added, are either deranged, Quixotic utopians, or perfidious liars. In the cosmic scheme of things, humans are not worth more than a pig, an ant, a rhinoceros, a platypus, or an iguana. Seen from that perspective, all life is precious, which is why we relentlessly, uncomprehendingly, malign it, cheapen it, erode it, stifle it. I had learned that lesson as a boy in German-occupied France. It was a lesson that would take on a whole new dimension when I crossed the Atlantic on my way to the "New World."

"He looked sadly down at the street,
as though it were his own bottomless sadness."
— Amerika, Franz Kafka (1883-1940)

IN THE BEGINNING—Memory is the time machine that takes us to the outer limits of our conscious selves. January 30, 1956. It was a winter dawn heavy with clouds the color of anger. Frost had formed overnight, and patches of rime speckled the promenade deck railing where I stood, an unknown emptiness adding to a flurry of tangled emotions.

I'd awakened early and clambered up on deck to see the Statue of Liberty, ready to weep with ritual if utterly unfelt reverence, eager to surrender like a pilgrim at a holy shrine to its symbolism and physicality. But the androgynous, vacant-eyed, stone-faced, copper-clad monolith had loomed across the bow, risen against the drab grayness of New York's concrete piers, fuming smokestacks, and decaying wooden hangars, then receded on the port side. To my dismay, the titan elicited none of the prescribed emotions or susceptibilities. I found it stiff, aloof. It lacked the stirring vigor or fabled grace I had envisioned. I'd often glimpsed absent-mindedly its diminutive twins, one under the chestnut trees in Paris' Jardin du Luxembourg where I played as a child, the other perched on a battlement overlooking the Seine River. Both, I thought—my sense of observation now betrayed—exuded more charisma, if not majesty, than the square-jawed icon with the Sphinx-like gaze towering above New York Harbor.

"Amerika! Amerika!" cried out an old man as he surveyed the unfolding scenery. He was at my elbow by the railing on the promenade deck. I'd not seen him draw near. His hands were clasped against his chest the way people hail a miracle or flinch before a great calamity. He was shaking his head from side to side as if his eyes and soul were not yet in sync. Gaunt, weather-

7

beaten, a week-old ashen stubble adding age to his years, he seemed to be inhaling the colossal spectacle, the unimaginable immensity that New York casts. Every pore, every crevice that carved his brow spoke of life endured, hopes deflected, fears surmounted and now, it seemed, dreams fulfilled. I would have given anything to share in his exhilaration, to consecrate with tears of gratitude my own ascension to the Promised Land.

"Yes, America," I echoed without joy, startled, and dismayed to find myself at its portal. Idealized and reinvented, perhaps to guard against its unfathomable essence, half- lusted, half-feared like a forbidden fruit, America had been but one of a thousand magical islands in a huge archipelago of youthful fantasies, Yesterday, in the unbroken vastness of a steel-blue Atlantic, America had been in the future. Yesterday there was a tomorrow to anticipate, a reality yet unconsummated among a stockpile of nebulous expectations. It was an indwelling, irreducible *now* that I faced as New York's colossal skyline dissolved into a nether realm of vapor and shadows and ghostly vessels heaving in the channel's inky waters.

The man grabbed my wrist and sobbed, *"Amerika, can it be? I waited so long."*

"Now look, sir," I wanted to tell the man, "It's adventure I seek, not sanctuary. Yes, I'm nomad, restless vagrant, incurable drifter, a Wandering Jew beguiled by locomotion, a Gypsy craving new horizons, a vagabond enlivened not by landings but by ceaseless migrations, a wayfarer steering not toward the nearest port of call but chasing after the open sea on a journey without end. I am all that, I grant you. Like my father before me, I roam, seeking both uniformity and self-regeneration through change, finding constancy and coherence in mutability, endlessly coveting a foretaste of the things only anticipation infers. But I am no refugee, I tell you, no battered remnant of war, and I resent that I might be mistaken for one. Unhand me, please."

But I said nothing. I didn't have the heart. A youthful insolence still percolating through my veins, traumatized by the inexplicable reality in which I'd suddenly been drawn, I needed to distance myself from this tempest-tossed wretched refuse who, like millions, had reached the golden door of America's promise. I ambled instead to the starboard side, the overcoat my parents had purchased a fortnight earlier no match against the arctic chill. Manhattan's ramparts rose before me, a monochrome carcass, unreal, grotesque in its breadth and bulk, and rendered more forbidding as memories of Paris, my beloved hometown, submerged my mind's eye with tears. I blamed the wind. I didn't want the man to think that they were tears of relief or elation.

I was 19.

Where am I? I rewind my life. Two years earlier, as I attended the Paris University School of Journalism, 70 simultaneous terrorist incidents against the French in Algeria turned a smoldering struggle for independence into an all-out war. France moved the bulk of its Foreign Legion troops to Algeria. Regular army conscripts followed. Soon, anecdotal accounts and isolated eyewitness reports of gross misbehavior by the French army surfaced in France, as did carefully filtered news of high casualty rates among French soldiers. The Algerians, who fought fiercely and lost over half a million people during the eight-year conflict, showed no mercy for the French they captured.

A legend cultivated by French revisionists 60 years after the end of a very bloody war asserts that Algeria was French. No. Algeria was a miserable colony whose citizens—about ten million—were held in a humiliating stranglehold of political, economic, social, and cultural inferiority by an elite of less than a million French settlers for more than a century. Yes, France built schools and hospitals, but most Algerians did not enjoy the rights or privileges granted their master colonizers. The degradation felt by the colonized stemmed less from the iniquity of their circumstances than from the symbolic and real rank of inferiority imposed by the usurper. The splitting of colonial society into two divergent domains — the conqueror and the conquered — lasted until the 1962. Algerian Jews were granted French citizenship, but it was denied to Muslims who were also banned from the ballot boxes. When rigged elections triggered demonstrations, kidnappings and extrajudicial executions followed.

Shortly before, France, soon to be replaced by an America afflicted with anti-*"communist"* hysteria, had abandoned Indochina following a bitter and futile campaign that culminated in a scathing defeat at Dien Bien Phu. The French debacle in its colonies of Vietnam, Laos, and Cambodia, and its loss of prestige internationally, ignited nationalist fervor among the French, especially those born in Algeria who considered it their own. France dispatched a large contingent of Foreign Legionnaires; army conscripts followed. Accounts of misbehavior by French soldiers circulated freely, as was the disturbing revelation that many French had been massacred. It was also learned that Algerian women had been raped, that men were beaten, immersed in icy water, showered with excrement, and electrocuted (a treatment that my late father, a member of the French Résistance, endured at the hands of the French Gestapo during his arrest at Fresnes Prison, France's second-largest penitentiary). Declassified documents, including photos and a glut of press reports, books, and documentaries continue to shed light on the atrocities committed by the French in Algeria. Refusing to admit defeat, the Algerians fought valiantly. The hostilities ended with the independence of Algeria and the dismembering of the French colonial empire. Many in France still mourn the loss of Algeria which, predictably, they blame on a *"communist"* conspiracy.

♦

Maurice Papon (1910-2007) is remembered as the secretary general of the Bordeaux police during the Second World War. He took part in the deportation of more than 1,600 Jews. He is also known to have tortured insurgent Algerian prisoners. Inexplicably, he was elected to several high-ranking ministerial positions after the war. In 1998, following a long investigation and protracted legal wranglings, he was eventually tried and convicted of crimes against humanity. He was released from prison early, in 2002, for "ill health." He died at home five years later.

So long as lions don't have their own historians, the history of hunting will always glorify the hunter.

♦

Determined to keep me from becoming a statistic, my mother urged that I be dispatched to America. My father demurred at first, arguing that I should not be encouraged to run from risk or responsibility.

"Who's to say he won't face the same perils in America," he asked. "Is America immune from war? The world is forever teetering on the brink of catastrophe. War lurks at every turn. Millions are immolated at the altar of ideology," he sighed, mourning the murder of his parents and two brothers in one of Hitler's extermination camps.

"He's just a boy," pleaded my mother. "He's bound to be drafted any day now. If they ship him to Algeria, he could be hurt—or worse."

My father frowned and stroked his forehead as if to brush away a hideous thought.

"You're right."

The truth, the sad truth is that I would be shipped to America, alone, not to seek my fortune but to evade near-certain service in Algeria where the French were dying like flies. I was headed to a New World I had never hankered and whose symbols, traditions, and doctrines would forever stand in stark contrast with the old world I came from. I wasn't fleeing persecution or indigence. I was quite happy living in Paris, a city that delights the eye and indulged the hedonist in me. It would be a long and bumpy ride to penury and everlasting regret.

There was another reason. I was doing poorly in school. "It's not the writing," the school chancellor explained in a letter to my parents:

"He can write. It's the rest — spotty attendance, unfinished assignments, a penchant for rabble-rousing, and an immoderate fondness for the opposite sex. Your son has been a constant distraction. We showed patience and restraint. We were lenient. When leniency failed, we took stiffer action, all for naught. Your son is smart but headstrong, gifted but undisciplined. He resents authority. He is not a team player. In time, perhaps, these shortcomings will abate. Meanwhile, we regret we cannot encourage you to enroll him for the coming term."

*"Bureaucracy: three fourths parasitic
and the other fourth stupid fumbling."*
— Robert A. Heinlein (1907-1988)

ADULTERY, FORNICATION, SODOMY. To supplement my parents' modest monthly stipend (and help subsidize my nightly outings to the plebeian whorehouses of Montmartre), I worked part-time as a foot messenger, ferrying mail and unclassified documents between the U.S. Embassy on Avenue Gabriel and the U.S. Information Service on Rue St. Honoré. The job kept me mostly outdoors, which I enjoyed. It was the behavior of my superiors—bilious third-echelon paper-pushers—that I resented. Hard as I tried to read them, to distill from alternating states of studied aloofness, self-importance, and irascibility some redeeming trait, the Americans with whom I rubbed elbows remained distant and impenetrable. What I did learn is that Americans treat foreigners as *"aliens,"* even when the aliens happen to be in their own country.

With the rest of the immigration paperwork out of the way, I was summoned to the U.S. Consulate for a final interview. The consul general, a diminutive, overbearing bureaucrat visibly luxuriating in his American-in-Paris dream job, handed me one last form, a three-section affidavit that he watched me read, fill out, and sign with roguish amusement.

I first had to swear that I'd not engaged in *"adultery, fornication, or sodomy."* I invited my inquisitor to define each of these infractions. He complied with clinical precision. Probing my political convictions, the second section asked whether I was *"now or had ever been a member of the Communist Party."* The third inquired whether it was my intention *"to cause the overthrow of the government of the United States by unconstitutional means."* Having answered all the above in the negative and so affirmed with one hand on the Bible, I was issued an immigration visa and granted

13

entry into the Promised Land. I would soon discover that in America, the most sex-obsessed nation on earth, promiscuity thrives in the very lap of puritanism, that organizations such as the John Birch Society, the Ku Klux Klan and Opus Dei—later the Family Research Council, Gun Owners of America, the Center for Immigration Studies, the Neo-Confederates, and other "alt-right" factions, are far more malignant than the atrophied French "Communist" Party, and that the U.S. Constitution is routinely circumvented or violated thanks to loopholes and legal acrobatics that allow the privileged and the powerful to defy the rule of law.

Yet unpolluted by such insights, I bid farewell to my parents. I left Paris on a cold, rainy mid-winter morning and arrived in Cannes that same evening. After a sleepless night, I embarked on the SS Constitution for the ten-day crossing to New York. I had fifty dollars in my coat pocket which my mother had dutifully sewn shut.

Lured by the siren call of adventure, I tried to mute the voices within. I would have cheerfully consigned America to that special region of the mind where fantasy and metaphor reside. Why, the voices intoned, couldn't America have been a vague eventuality instead of a destination? All rivers spring from a source. All events have a cause. Every event sets off a cascade of unforeseen events. The process is unceasing, and the permutations are endless. In a sense all events are related. In apprehending these verities, I was taught a lesson that was both axiomatic and unlearnable.

I watched France's coastline recede in the distance and I wept.

♦

Where am I? I rewind my life. January 30, 1956. New York towers above me, gray, dank, alien, menacing, as I shiver on the promenade deck of the SS Constitution. I try to make sense of this latest disembodiment; I resent my parents who sent me here—for my own good, they assured me; I'm ashamed of the docility with which I acquiesced to this expatriation. Driven by an age-old momentum, in search of new horizons, convinced that permanency can be attained only through change, I'd embarked on what I'd hoped to be a life of serene itinerancy. I found myself marooned instead on the inhospitable shores of an ideologically divided realm that preaches love in its temples and practices hatred on its streets and battlefields.

> *"That's why they call it the American Dream,*
> *because you have to be asleep to believe it."*
> **— George Carlin (1937-2008)**

THE PROMISED LAND—I turn the pages and peel memories like an onion. Post-war America: Industrious, affluent, smug, brimming with hope. A family of four lived comfortably on a single wage-earner's salary. If you lost your job today, you could find a better one tomorrow. Of course, America is incurably racist, xenophobic, a swamp of exceptionalism and entitlement, its people quick to do battle in other people's back yards (the latest in a long list of crippling debacles in Afghanistan where, for nearly twenty years, the U.S. was at war with the truth and stranded without an end-game strategy).[1] Employers could fire women for getting pregnant, women had no legal right to a harassment-free workplace, they were charged extra for health insurance, and could be legally raped by their husbands. But the dollar had weight and worth. "Made in the USA" spelled excellence. A car cost $2,000; a gallon of gas — 23 cents. You could buy a decent house for $22,000. Sensing that foreign policy is strictly about power and narrow interests President *"I like Ike"* Dwight D. Eisenhower warned against the evils of the military-industrial complex and the lure of armed entanglements, while economists and social scientists cautioned against the very excesses that, six decades later, would turn the U.S. into a mafia state dedicated to enriching a privileged few by emasculating a once thriving middle class and driving the poor into an abyss of privation and despair.

If a system is built on power but lacks legitimacy, behaviorists warned, it will destroy itself. If it asserts moral

---

[1] A confidential trove of government documents obtained by The Washington Post reveals that senior U.S. officials failed to tell the truth about the war in Afghanistan throughout the 18-year campaign, issuing rosy reports they knew to be false and hiding evidence that the war had become unwinnable.

truths but lacks the power to enforce them, it will unravel. Their counsel fell on deaf ears.

◆

Meanwhile, Elvis *"the pelvis"* Presley scandalized pedants and prudes with his hit single, *Hound Dog*, but no one recoiled when, fiercely opposed to integration, 101 members of Congress signed the racist Southern Manifesto. Nor would anyone be shocked to learn, after his death in 2003, that South Carolina Senator Strom Thurmond, the self-confessed bigot who co-authored the manifesto, had fathered a child with his Black maid.

Schools, lunch counters, public toilets, and water fountains were segregated. Blacks were consigned to the back of the bus. They were often lynched, arrested on trumped-up charges, wrongly convicted and imprisoned, humiliated, and dehumanized. Many, after spending years on death row, were executed because white justice never was, is not, can never be, color-blind. But what the hell, if you were white and had a steady job, life in these United States was a bowl of cherries. Given capitalism's all-consuming gluttony, for a growing number of Americans, white, black, and brown, the bowl of cherries has since turned into a vat of shit in which we are now all drowning.

Relaxed, playful, upbeat, frivolous, given to good-natured inanity—as witnessed by the dim-witted feel-good "beach" movies it released that decade—America began baring its soul and hinted at the anxieties, the fretful self-inquiry to which it would later succumb as the world began to unravel. Hollywood turned introspective: *East of Eden*; *Rebel Without a Cause*; *The Blackboard Jungle*; *The Bad Seed*; *The Wild One*; *Marty*. Orwell published his prescient dystopia, *1984*. The great Tennessee Williams shoved a mirror in America's face. His plays, later made into movies—*On the Waterfront*; *A Streetcar Named Desire*;

Cat on a Hot Tin Roof; Suddenly Last Summer; The Night of the Iguana; and Sweet Bird of Youth—pointed fingers at America's greed, superficiality, political sleaze, lies, decadence, and sexual depravity; they lashed out at insanity, the absurdity of life, and the inevitability of death. All echoed feelings of unease first articulated in the internal dialogues of a nation stirring from hubristic complacency to vigilance, from presumed invincibility to perceived vulnerability and willing, at least for now, to shed its ill-fitting and deceptive disguise. But the small screen, which now holds America captive, retaliated. The strong, silent bronc-bustin' pistol-packin' cigarillo-chompin' Bourbon-chuggin' enforcer who rides into the sunset was now idolized. The desperado, a tragic figure who evokes inexplicable sympathy, always got it in the end. *Gunsmoke, The Virginian, Wagon Train, Rawhide, Have Gun: Will Travel, The Rifleman, Bonanza*, and *High Noon* all reminded audiences of their "heroic" past and reanimated a nostalgia for that lawless epoch. One is not surprised to learn that upon visiting the U.S. in 1882, Irish poet and playwright, Oscar Wilde (1854-1900) famously wrote in a letter:

> *"Americans are certainly hero-worshipers, and always take their heroes from the criminal classes."*

◆

The Sixties and Seventies ushered an era oxygenated by the rise of an ebullient counterculture. Emancipated from the phony primness of the finicky Fifties, hastily cleansed from the obscenity of McCarthyism, sickened by the Vietnam War, the Kent State massacre, and the Watergate scandal, America welcomed the Beatles, let its hair down, burned draft cards, set fire to ROTC buildings and donned Nehru jackets, dashikis, and beaded necklaces. Malcolm X electrified his people and shocked white America. Black Panther founder and co-author (with

Bobby Seale) of the Party's 10-point manifesto, Huey Newton, who would be assassinated in 1989, Eldridge Cleaver and comedian Dick Gregory, the eloquent drum major for civil rights, parlayed acerbic tongue and mordant wit into a brand of social activism that bolstered black America's selfhood. Back from Paris where he was welcomed and cheered, James Baldwin rose from obscurity to become a commanding literary icon. Also back from Paris, where she blossomed and honed an emergent sense of justice, Sartre scholar and one of the FBI's Ten Most Wanted Fugitives, Angela Davis, took America by storm. A cultural phenomenon, Alex Haley's *Roots* offered, for the first time, a Back perspective of life in Africa and unerringly recorded the bestiality of slavery. In Kunta Kinte are incarnated the horrors and heroism of the Black experience. Lenny Bruce, Mort Sahl, and George Carlin turned humor on its head. Their irreverence and biting political satire challenged an outwardly straitlaced but dissolute society and helped redefine and broaden free speech. Jack Kerouac, the leading chronicler of the *"beat generation"* [he coined the term] shocked America with autobiographical sketches that reflect deep social angst assuaged by drugs, alcohol, spiritualism, and scorching wit. His leading apostle, Allen Ginsberg, vented his rage against capitalism with a tortured lyricism kindled by LSD. Flower children preached love, not war. *Oh! Calcutta*, memorable for its brazen displays of frontal nudity, male and female, and *Hair*, the tribal love-rock musical, opened to rave reviews. The plays would enthrall audiences for years to come. This was an era of rebellious sex and drugs and freedom from the shackles of social conformity while *"Christofascism,"* a neologism coined by German liberation theologist Dorothee Sölle in 1970 that describes the intersection and merging between fascism and Christianity was rearing its ugly head). It was a time of nascent impiety and growing suspicion of the political structures that Americans take for granted, an age long remembered and still reviled by the straitlaced hypocrites who lived through it and mourned the adulteration of their precious white, Anglo-Saxon, Protestant paradise.

I watched these transformations with a relish that did not foster in me an urge to partake. I inwardly rejoiced at the consternation these upheavals seemed to wreak upon America's squeamish psyche, but I espoused none of the causes they championed or spawned, at least not openly. I didn't let my hair grow until long hair was passé. I cut it short the moment manes were back in vogue. I sported a beard when facial hair went out of style; I shaved it off as soon as hirsute faces outnumbered beardless ones. I snubbed the fashions of the day — polyester leisure suits and wide psychedelic neckties and bandanas and bell-bottom trousers and high-heeled clogs and anti-bomb symbols. I used none of the jargon, neologisms, and prevailing affectations. I *"dropped out"* on my own time, at my own pace, disinclined to assert my individuality by rushing to embrace someone else's conformist eccentricities. Purely academic, my fascination for the politics of dissent remained voyeuristic. I refused to get involved for fear that doing so would dilute the thrill of spectatorship. But I was elated. For a time, I thought that having identified the real enemy, young progressives and old radicals would lock arms, learn how to fight, and push for meaningful reforms. I was wrong. Reality outdid my most fervent expectations. When capitalism is the enemy, its ideological opposite doesn't have a prayer.

◆

America is no monolith. Viewed from a distance, however, it matches the caricature-like image much of the world has formed: a nation that forswore all princes and potentates in exchange for the majesty (and illusion) of self-rule—but capitulated to the czars of capital]; a theocentric nation hooked on triumphalism, given to gluttonous mercantilism and bulimic consumerism, a goliath beguiled by its grandiose self-view and readily seduced by the idolatrous slogans it keeps coining in its own name; a hulk obsessed with bigness: wall-sized television screens, mega churches, a goliath enamored of pistols and assault rifles, souped-up, gas-guzzling SUVs and giant pickup trucks, super-sized meals, a *"He-man"* whose propensity for violence is taken to the limit in *"expeditionary"* wars and *"armed interventions"* aimed to force democracy in places that never had it and have no use for it.

Of Americans, I deduced a sanguine, gregarious, and resourceful lot prone to frivolity and hero worship—thespians and crooners, many of dubious talent, fictional celluloid *übermenschen*, comely people of both genders, sports figures, many of them otherwise unremarkable human beings who but for their height, brawn, or dexterity with some implement (a ball, club, stick or pair of boxing gloves) and blaring divas whose renown rests entirely on their unearned celebrity, their udders, and the amplitude of their gyrating buttocks—all of whom would be living in obscurity instead of being lionized and earning obscenely high wages.

At their finest, Americans are generous to a fault. At their worst, they're annoyingly trivia-driven, provincial, blinkered, outwardly cocksure, inwardly skittish, overindulged, overfed, oversexed, and combative. Reared to idolize and emulate vulgar hoodlums—otherwise referred to as *"folk heroes"* (Daniel Boone, Davy Crocket, George Armstrong Custer, Buffalo Bill, Kit Carson, and Wyatt Earp), the men are high-strung, sexually conflicted, homophobic, and touchy. Bursting with testosterone, they are desperately protective of their masculinity, enamored of their pickup trucks, and enraptured by their guns, which they keep lovingly oiled, loaded, and cocked. Women are prematurely pubescent, no doubt the victims of the food industry's use of toxic additives that increase the shelf life of their otherwise tasteless commodities. As they age, many develop neuroses resulting from exposure to American men who, unlike their sexually emancipated European counterparts, are raised to be emotionally unavailable macho males. Together, they produce children who grow up into a me-generation of arrogant, narcissistic, self-preening selfie-takers bursting with gluttonous egos who want "it" all and want it *now!*

Of course, they take *social* studies in school, are taught *social* graces, are influenced by *Social* Darwinism, claw their way up the *social* ladder and, having reached to top, hire *social* secretaries who handle *social* calendars brimming with *social* obligations. Overly *sociable*, some come down with *social* diseases. All eventually become eligible for *Social* Security. Somehow, none takes umbrage at the word "social" except when twinned with the word "medicine" which, Great Zeus, suddenly transmutes into some ungodly obscenity, a "communist" plot, the anti-Christ in the flesh. This is a form of virulent logophobia (an irrational fear of certain words) transmitted by misguided propagandists and blithely spread by idiots who savor the five-day, eight-hour-a-day workweek, the right to unionize, unemployment insurance, Workers' Compensation, Social Security, and other "socialist" New Deal initiatives. For most, the "truth" is what they perceive or what they've been brainwashed to believe. Which is why fundamental truths are drowning in an ocean of lies while other "truths" are being manufactured to suit social trends or meet the needs of conspiracy theorists and would-be dictators.

◆

To those who suggest that America has changed in the past 66 years, I submit that it is just more revealed: It was always a charismatic fraudster; it eventually bared its tainted soul when

Barack Hussein Obama ran for president, was elected, and reelected to a second term. Who can forget protest signs showing a white-faced and bloody-mouthed Obama as a satanic clown, or as Hitler, complete with mustache and swastika? How odd that burning the flag is infuriating, but depicting an urbane, cultured, refined individual as a buffoon and a maniacal fascist is hailed as *"free speech."*

The ugly aftershocks and secessionist rants that Obama's victories and popularity generated, the deep current of racism coursing through America's veins, suggest that large numbers of Americans are bigoted, xenophobic, misogynous, and dementedly religious. The November 2014 mid-term elections, in which six of the most backsliding states helped Republicans regain control of the Senate, tend to validate this premise. In America's first black commander-in-chief, they now saw a symbol of their nation's increasing diversity. That "transformation," which would inspire the *"Great Replacement"* theory scared the hell out of them. The potential for racially motivated violence was never higher, as mushrooming far-right terrorism and a string of police-involved incidents would demonstrate.

◆

The 80s and 90s brought fleeting professional achievements, prolonged setbacks, and personal ordeals. I travelled. I wrote. Good jobs and good money gave way to lengthy periods of unemployment and indigence interrupted by brief stints at dull or profitless occupations. Joblessness soared during the Reagan years. In 1982, 30 million Americans were out of work. I was one of them. I lost my medical insurance, as did 16 million others. At 45, I felt the sting of *"over-qualification,"* the dastardly ploy to replace mature, tenured, skilled employees with younger, cheaper labor. The specter of chronic unemployment loomed ahead, menacing, pitiless. Benefits dried up, pushing untold numbers of citizens to the brink.

As working Americans struggled to survive, huge sums of taxpayer dollars were raised to finance pork barrel projects and wars. In defiance of a law prohibiting the U.S. from supporting, directly or indirectly, military, and paramilitary operations in Nicaragua, the Reagan administration flouted the edict and secretly subsidized a right-wing guerrilla force known as the "Contras," looking for "third-party" support, namely from Iran. Reagan personally solicited funds from Saudi Arabia to the tune of $32 million. Cesspools of corruption awash in human rights abuses, Guatemala and Honduras served as conduits in the traffic of weapons and drugs to the anti-Sandinista rebels.

Then the Soviet empire collapsed. Following two visits to Moscow during which Russia transitioned from illusory "communism" to sham democracy, I diagnosed the Russian people in an article published in the March 1991 edition of Penthouse titled *The Opium of Perestroika* as "suffering from cancer of the soul." I had written:

"...Born from an ideological crisis, incapable of dusting off the web of Stalinism. Perestroika had failed to ensure liberty, to kindle abundance, to hasten the end of economic stagnation, to inspire social equilibrium. The new Russian classes faced an insurmountable problem: Perestroika, the powerful instrument of social destabilization, had not yet learned to become an instrument of social conservation. Thus, miracles, like hot water or uninterrupted electric and telephone service or fully stocked grocery shelves, will continue to be transient phenomena. After all, too much of a good thing risks corrupting the masses."

U.S. foreign policy, no longer forged in the crucible of Cold War paranoia, was now animated by a fear of incipient foreign nationalism and rebellions fueled by ethnic and religious factionalism, poverty, government sleaze and apathy, and deepening despair. Noam Chomsky remarked:

> *"The appeal to security* [is] *largely fraudulent, the Cold War framework having been used as a device to justify the oppression of independent nationalism."*

Indeed, nascent foreign nationalism was a threat to a precious few: Anaconda Copper, United Fruit/Chiquita Banana, Dole, International Telephone and Telegraph, Coca Cola, PepsiCo, General Electric, Aramco, IBM, and other giant corporations and lending institutions that enrich themselves and their stockholders by systematically sucking the economic marrow of poor nations.

◆

A new century dawned, a new millennium began full of illusive promises and fanciful auguries. The flower children and the anti-war protestors of my youth grew into flabby, self-absorbed, cantankerous septuagenarians. Their once raised, clenched fists are down, the voices of dissent, the cries for peace are now but feeble bleats. I lament my cynicism and noninvolvement at a time when America's youth bravely denounced injustice and chicanery, when they marched against ignoble wars and poured scorn on ignoble leaders while other young Americans died far from home as lies and colossal fraud were being heaped on a nation too smug to care.

The American Dream, I would soon discover is a vast exaggeration, a myth whose advent and incarnation are reserved for the privileged and resourceful few who know how to play the game, pull strings, exploit loopholes, bend the rules, and milk the system. Once a middle-class society with professed core values of hard work, opportunity, and fair play, the U.S. was now being submerged under a tsunami of right-wing economic, political, and religious influences. The victim of corporate greed, its bourgeoisie was frittering away. With the explosive growth of the radical right—fueled by fears generated by economic dislocation and demonizing conspiracy theories—white Christian hate groups proliferated and vented their bile against changing racial demographics and, notably, the election of the first Black president. An angry backlash against what political and religious conservatives perceived as the *"socialization"* of America spawned the monsters of Islamophobia, anti-intellectualism, censorship, racial profiling, police brutality, and a form of jingoism that openly condones—or cheers—the use of torture.

Despite the strident hoopla, America was *not*:

• Invincible. The U.S. lost in Korea, Vietnam, Somalia, Iraq, and Afghanistan where it was held hostage for 20 years; it "triumphed"—at a cost—against tiny Grenada and Panama. Meanwhile, covert operations, drone strikes, electronic surveillance and stealth engagements led by black ops units, mercenary armies, and terrorist groups, are now common tools of U.S. foreign policy. Since the end of World War II, the U.S. had undertaken over 300 military "interventions," deploying troops to stamp out "communism" or overthrow regimes hostile to U.S. economic or strategic interests. Trump's lies and crudities have since given wings to the idea that the U.S. is an exceptional nation entitled to rule the world.

• The sponsor of democracy. The U.S. ranks 20th, trailing Norway, Iceland, Denmark, Sweden, New Zealand, and Australia.

• A guiding light of spiritual objectivity. Americans ignore or abet the incestuous tryst between the body politic and the dinosaurs of the religious right. Considered the greatest threat to the constitutionally mandated separation of church and state, the nation's largest religious right organizations continue to amass political power and wealth while stimulating and sharpening conservative angst. Together, as they muscle in on the body politic, these groups raise more than a billion dollars annually and invest large sums designed to inject religion into public schools.

• A paragon of moral probity. America fakes puritanism and wallows in scarlet promiscuity and vice. Americans self-righteously denounce abortion but cheer when a condemned man is hanged, roasted on the electric chair, or writhes in agony as he is injected with a lethal cocktail of drugs.

• The custodian of a free press. What we have are faint-hearted mainstream media beholden first and foremost to its advertisers; a press that won't challenge the evisceration of civil liberties; won't protest against the enfeeblement of the middle class; won't acknowledge that a huge number of Americans barely survive on starvation wages; won't denounce the consolidation of wealth into ever-narrowing circles of corporate power; will censure neither racism, the right wing's blitz against labor nor condemn the obscene cost of food and life-saving medicines, nor denounce a dysfunctional and predatory healthcare system ranked 37th (after Costa Rica, Saudi Arabia and Malta! France is still No. 1). The result of a glut of media-driven mythmaking, the rift between reality and reporting has ended. Widening, the credibility gap, according to Sonoma University sociology professor, Peter Phillips, it [has]

"... turned into a literal truth emergency ... the result of phony elections, illegal preemptive wars, extraordinary rendition, torture camps, doctored intelligence and issues that intimately impact our lives at home, from healthcare to education."

Clearly this truth emergency stems from the failures of the Fourth Estate to serve as the nation's free and outspoken conscience. Meanwhile, America was merrily sauntering down a primrose path of media-driven revivalism. Corporate mainstream media organizations, the pundits they sponsor and manipulate, and politicians from both parties (each the flipside of the same tarnished coin), composed a new contextual refrain: *"On September 11, 2001, everything changed."* From cable television to AM radio, from the blogosphere to town-hall meetings, Americans were being repeatedly told: *"This is a post-9/11 world."*

Many Americans have since surmised that *"everything"* did not change. Corporate media have resurrected powerful legends from the nation's past to shape public perception. In fact, the media are doing more mythmaking than investigative reporting. Even before it became a nation, the U.S. relied heavily on cultural mythology to instill in its citizens a sense of history, meaning, and purpose. As their needs changed, Americans told themselves new stories; they spun new fables.

Runaway capitalism continues to underwrite America's incestuous relations with autocratic or quasi-democratic nations around the world and keeps stoking war fever. To maintain the juggernaut's momentum while doubts over the purpose and direction of conflicts widen, the Pentagon is addressing a growing recruitment problem by spending billions of taxpayer dollars on programs designed to deceive, seduce, and capture the youth of America. U.S. conduct at home and abroad contributes to the mounting suspicion by friends and foes alike that America speaks with a forked tongue and acts solely in its own political and hegemonic interests.

Chinks are developing in America's bubble. Perspicacious citizens are beginning to note with noticeable unease that the U.S. does not and never did resemble the fabled image it has of itself, but that it has instead turned into an opportunistic, self-indulgent, arrogant, and sanctimonious empire soon to morph into a tightly controlled (spied on]) feudal society consisting of immensely rich dynasties and increasingly larger castes of serfs doomed to a life of bondage and penury. While it retains the trappings of a tolerant democracy, with perfunctory elections and an obliquely elected body of legislators, its institutions are alarmingly hollow and corruptible, and their power springs from deep-pocketed corporate elites. America is jumpy, angry, increasingly violent, and morally bankrupt. More and more citizens are struggling to survive and, as several socio-economic indicators foretell, they will face even harder times ahead.

One must be extraordinarily well off in America to safeguard one's assets. Average workers can barely keep their heads above water and an inequitable taxation system makes sure they can never climb out of it. Every dollar they put in a savings account has already been taxed. Why are they being taxed a second time for conducting what amounts to a private transaction with a financial institution? Why are their earnings so fraudulently assessed when corporate giants pay no taxes at all? Why do CEOs receive millions of dollars in yearly bonuses and the steel worker who erects skyscrapers has zero say in how his tax dollars are being spent? Why are there no cash reserves to subsidize and resurrect moribund cultural institutions, build schools, and feed the poor, but plenty of money to fund illegal and unwinnable wars, to bankroll trips to the Moon and Mars when Earth is ailing from neglect and abuse, and to keep some 1.5 million troops stationed in 150 countries around the world?

Once a leader in the humanities, America has since cut funds to education and the arts. Its infrastructures are crumbling. Roads and bridges are in a state of shocking disrepair; schools, hospitals, mental institutions are closing at an alarming rate (but for-profit prisons are bursting at the seams). There are four times more high school dropouts than in 1956 when I first arrived in America, and those who graduate can't spell, can't name the vice president, can't find Australia on a world map, and have no idea who won the Civil War — or why it was fought. Math grades continue to plummet. A climate of anti-intellectualism, anti-erudition prevails. America's love affair with guns is a form of osmotic psychosis unrelated to the ill-conceived 18th century statute that has since been hijacked by the gun lobby and sanctified by gun fetishists. What is it about their temperament that convinces Americans they are entitled to own guns? Surely, it's not just a poorly worded and myopic codicil penned in 1791.

My assessment of America is not one in which I take pleasure. Alas, as time passes, I find more evidence to support it. If America only shed its affectations and conceded that its concept of *"liberty and justice for all"* is a farce, that during its gestation and after its birth as a nation it engaged in brutal acts of banditry, first against indigenous populations — which it damn nearly liquidated — then against the imported Black labor it enslaved for more than two centuries; that it waged wars of imperialism and economic colonization; that its wealth is based on ruthless capitalism and the enrichment of privileged classes ... then I would say, O.K., the problem is not America, it's human nature. But when a nation goes to such lengths to proclaim its invincibility, to trumpet its moral superiority, to vaunt its virtues as it wallows in depravity, when it pompously grants itself the right to tell the rest of the world what to think and how to behave, when it meddles in other people's affairs in the name of *"national security,"* (a slogan that must be understood to mean the safety of top-ranking government officials, wealthy elites, and financial institutions); when it ships the flower of its youth to die, be maimed or rendered mad in illegal, immoral, and unwinnable wars ... then it's not human nature anymore; it's a national mindset, a mentality, an attitude, a strange and troubling ingrained societal trait. A superpower that professes moral arguments to buttress its global vision for civil liberties and democracy cannot just abandon those standards in its senseless search for absolute hegemony.

Of course, America has its amiable side. So long as I behave like an American (or pretend to) it grants me the right not to feel like one. But there is an art to *being* an American, a subliminal skill that can be acquired only at birth, then sharpened in the crucible of America's self-promoting culture. *Becoming* an American is infinitely harder. For some the effort and the inevitable transformations that ensue are their own supreme reward. Others, like me, get lost in the shuffle. The moorings that once linked me to the past where my selfhood resides are frayed. Surrendered to a wasteland of unending transience and irresolution, I'm reduced to mimicking the world around me. I follow the script, mouth the lines, control my inflection, and trim my body language, all with mock self-assurance but without the slightest conviction. It's quite an act.

I shall not fault America for having failed to match a set of fanciful assumptions brought to these shores by a wide-eyed adolescent and clung to because they once fit my model of Eldorado. Hard as I tried to resist America's lures, I've since become habituated to its creature comforts and extravagances but none of its customs, conventions, and convictions. Perhaps all I can hope for is an unstudied acquiescence to things as they are, a piecemeal accommodation with the subtle inhibitions and tempting inducements that are part of the American experience.

At the end of the day (literally, not figuratively as the pompous halfwits who mean to say *"eventually,"* not late afternoon, evening, dusk, twilight, sunset, or the dead of night) and after an exhausting trek through assorted minefields, I retreat backstage, wipe off the greasepaint, tuck away the libretto and sink within myself like into a soft, cozy armchair. Once ensconced in this reassuring setting, reverting to the common idiom in which I address myself, now safe in the lap of hindsight, I survey my inner world, thankful it is still there, neighborly and obliging. Some of the greasepaint, like a tattoo,

31

never comes off. Could I have become, by default, *malgré moi*, an American? The question, and the inferences it raises, leave me perplexed. All I know is that after years of a love-hate relationship with New York, I succumbed to its myriad enticements and became one of its greatest fans. I cannot say the same for the rest of America.

◆

And then, lo and behold, came Trump and his flying monkeys. I began to suspect that America's imaginary narrative (still vapidly described as an *"experiment"*) was ultimately dystopian, infused with questionable idealism, and lacking a strategic endgame other than defending its superpower status and protecting capitalism. As I watched, America, on edge, angry, was mutating into a mob.

> *"The deterioration of every government begins*
> *with the decay of the principles on which it was founded."*
> **—Montesquieu (1689-1755)**

ON "COMMUNISM" — Fast forward. May 2019. Year Three of Donald J. Trump's malignant presidency and less than five months before a novel corona virus, silent, invisible, deadly, and now believed to have been incubating in the damp shadows of a Chinese food market, took the world by storm and claimed its most vulnerable quarries. At the time, Trump's fulminating rhetoric, aberrations, threats, and reckless governance seemed to pose the greater danger. Vaccines against the dreaded pandemic had not yet been formulated and there seemed to be no antitoxin capable of neutralizing a wayward president and his henchmen's assault on democracy. Two months earlier, the U.S. military had killed dozens of people in Syria, including women and children, in airstrikes conducted during the final days of the war against the Islamic State, but did not disclose its actions for more than two years. According to the New York Times, military officials sought to conceal the strike, and multiple investigative reports scrutinizing what had happened were *"delayed, sanitized and classified."* It was a time of fear and anger and uncertainty best endured or sidelined far from the madding crowd in the insulating company of books.

◆

Yale University Professor Timothy D. Snyder's monumental epic, *Black Earth — The Holocaust as History and Warning,* is elegantly written and filled with timeless wisdom, jarring truths, and persuasive admonitions. The 2016 New York Times bestseller is not an easy read. Like good wine it must be sipped slowly. It is one of the most comprehensive studies on mass insanity, on the origins, rise, and evolution of totalitarianism, and a stark warning against its persistent appeal in a country that had once gone to war to crush it.

I remember questioning Professor Snyder's casual if not hasty use of the word "communism," a term I always write or utter flanked by quotation marks. Sadly, given man's cupidity and narcissism, the Marxist ideals that could have turned humanity into a family instead of ceaselessly warring factions never left the printed page. What passed for "communism," notably in Russia and Eastern Europe, China, and Cuba, was a heavy-handed, ruthless, tyrannical system of governance in which the individual is sacrificed at the altar of the party. The only locales where a semblance of the "communist" model has ever been successfully implemented are Israeli cooperatives (kibbutzim) and monasteries. I wish Snyder had made that distinction in his otherwise superb history and commentary on the extremist ideological threats that continue to face society.

In Senator Joseph McCarthy's America of the 1950s, freethinking, artistic non-conformity, secularism, and a penchant for social justice were also seen by far-right demagogues as "communist" plots. Popular liberation movements aimed at shaking the yoke of colonialism, Liberation Theology (viewed as a *"cancer in the Church"* by Christianity's hardliners), and efforts by labor to unionize were vilified, as would those who opposed U.S. military *"interventions."* Incomprehensibly, John Lennon's pro-peace Platonic activism was also attributed to *"communist leanings"* that his accusers knew to be false. Had they lived today, Thomas Paine and the poet Henry David Thoreau would also be branded "communists." Recently, Canadian Prime Minister Justin Trudeau was called a "communist" by a phalanx of U.S. right-wing politicians for announcing a mandatory buyback program targeting assault weapons and new regulations that will ban sales and imports of handguns. The legislation, in response to the latest deadly mass shootings, is expected to pass.

The aggressive investment strategies and light-fingered manipulations that characterize capitalism are saluted as "entrepreneurial patriotism" even though they undermine the middle class and harm the poor. The Nazis, self-styled "communists," and the Church persecuted Freemasons. The Nazis accused them of being *"hostile to the State."* The paranoid Stalin called the ancient brotherhood *"an agent of Western imperialism."* Catholics, (and not a few Evangelical Christians) who have never set foot in a Masonic lodge, see it as *"blasphemous and satanic."* Two centuries earlier, ideas expounded by English and French philosophers, some of them Freemasonry's founding fathers, notably the belief that science and logic give people more knowledge and understanding than tradition and religion, were ruthlessly attacked by the Vatican. Pope Clement XII (1652-1740) issued a decree in which Freemasonry is described as *"a serious threat to the hegemony of the Church,"* no doubt because many early Freemasons were—as are their modern-day successors—agnostics and atheists. Several Freemasons were arrested, accused of heresy, subjected to torture, and burned alive at the stake. Everything is semantics. It takes scoundrels to corrupt language and idiots to lap up the lies the words conceal.

There is another problem. What passed for "communism" hopelessly perverted the virtues the paradigm embodies. Worse, it betrayed the ideals carefully crafted in Marx's *Das Kapital*, which calls for a classless society in which the means of production and the profits therefrom are shared equally. Instead of addressing urgent social problems—inequality, poverty, injustice, corruption, hunger, and illiteracy—the "communist" crusade resorted to an apostolate of terror that belied its Utopian fantasies while claiming millions of lives. Ultimately, the rules of the game of "communism," as are the sledgehammer dictates of religion, are unenforceable because they collide with human greed and egoism. There is much to regret about the dismal perversion of "communism's" objectives. Under the brutal stewardship of misguided disciples or turncoat falsifiers, Marx's magnificent folly failed. History will have to classify this failure, which cost some 100 million lives, as one of the greatest human tragedies and a sinister joke. In the hands of zealots, idealism turns to dogma, altruism veers toward selfishness, and the urge to serve a cause is often corrupted by the compulsion to manipulate it. Marx and co-author Friedrich Engels may have intended their writings to inspire hope in a downtrodden proletarian audience but theirs are works on economics, sociology and history that also address the nature, development, and dangers of the capitalist system. Russians called themselves "communists" in the wake of the 1917 revolution, but they misinterpreted (or perverted) both the term and the concept and produced a dictatorial horror that forever put an end to the "communist" dream.

"Communism" (or what would be hailed as an antidote for the ills of mankind) is a visionary and impracticable socio-economic and political concept that deepened the conflict between the ruling classes (the elites who control the means of production) and the proletariat who toil to enrich the elites. Employing a critical approach known as historical materialism, Karl Marx accurately predicted that capitalism promotes inequality and injustice but overlooked or miscalculated two dynamics: Capitalism's propensity to forgo the carrot and opt for the stick as a way of silencing its critics; and man's innate sense of entitlement. Instead of leading to therapeutic socialism, it used repression. Nor did Marx envisage what is now termed "catabolic capitalism," described by Craig Collins, a judge on the Judicial District Court in North Carolina as,

"... a self-cannibalizing system whose insatiable hunger for profit can only be fed by devouring the society that sustains it. As it rampages down the road to ruin, this system gorges itself on one self-inflicted disaster after another."

Capitalists will continue to gorge themselves on successive disasters and laugh all the way to the bank until this self-cannibalism has chewed, swallowed, and digested the last morsel of life on Earth. Imagine a hydra devouring itself. It's quite a spectacle, the last frenetic performance we will ever witness before the final curtain. To expect otherwise is a waste of time, energy, and precious emotional security.

Collectively understood as Marxism, Marx's critical theories about society, economics, and politics, failed. I spent years trying to explain to east European victims of "communism" that, say, members of Romania's Iron Guard, gangsters who turned overnight from ardent fascists into enthusiastic "communists" ... were NOT "communists." They were, before and after, unrepentant anti-Semites who promoted the idea that *"Rabbinical aggression against the Christian world"* — which manifests itself through Freemasonry, Freudianism, homosexuality, atheism, Marxism, and the civil war in Spain — were undermining society. They merely traded their olive-green uniforms or traditional peasant costumes adorned with crucifixes and bags of Romanian soil around their necks (to emphasize their commitment to authentic Romanian folk values), for red scarves. I also tried to make the case that those who genuinely believed themselves to be serving the collectivist cause were cruelly duped by an unworkable ideology so badly corrupted that they savagely turned against it. It was a huge waste of time. I'm having the same problem explaining this paradox to Americans. Their eyes glaze in total bewilderment. The obvious is often incomprehensible. You can call a chihuahua a descendent of the wolf but it's a stretch.

♦

Aroused and nurtured by a prevailing countercurrent of chauvinism, racism, and xenophobia, the "anticommunist" hysteria that was sweeping America soon merged with and fed the ravenous aims of global fascism. Left unchecked, I mused as I turned the last page of Snyder's haunting master work, America's growing flirtation with totalitarianism—inspired by its racist past and reinvigorated by Donald Trump's colossal fabrications and stupefyingly rabble-rousing oratory—could easily transform it into the terrifying white supremacist state many of its citizens seem to crave. My instincts, those of a Holocaust survivor, did not betray me.

What had transpired, three years into Trump's presidency, was premonitory and terrifying. A faction of scowling right-wing fanatics, in and out of government, bent on turning back the clock and restoring the Confederacy, slavery, and lynching, was now engaged in a frontal offensive on democracy. Two years earlier, Snyder's *On Tyranny: Twenty Lessons from the Twentieth Century*, had prophetically remarked:

> *"Fascists reject reason in the name of will, denying objective truth in favor of a glorious myth articulated by leaders who claim to give voice to the people… Most of the power of authoritarianism is freely given. In times like these, individuals think ahead about what a more repressive government will want, and then offer themselves without being asked. A citizen who adapts in this way is teaching power what to do. Anticipatory obedience is a political tragedy."*

Many Americans didn't just obey. They groveled and swooned and roared like idolaters before a golden calf and I saw in their robotic body language, the trance-like fury in their eyes, and the snarling rictus that twisted their jaws, the same frenzied passion, the same shared hallucination that stirred Hitler's adoring automatons. As these histrionics unfolded across the land, the pandemic claimed its own casualties while thermometers and medical grade alcohol disappeared from pharmacy shelves.

♦

Three years later, Snyder warned:

> *"The right-wing media, with a few honorable exceptions, is one giant safe space for the Big Lie. So, the reality-based press needs to make 'democracy the story,' because elements of the GOP are actively working to subvert future elections through laws, regulations, and propaganda efforts. "*

Snyder quite realistically described how a presidential loser could be cast as the winner in 2024:

> *"That is what's happening right before our eyes right now, and we're just too cowardly to look at it."*

Hadn't Florida Congressman Matt Gaetz and former Trump adviser Steve Bannon float the idea that an *"army of patriots and shock troops should be prepared to take over the government if the former president runs and wins in 2024"*? Deconstructed in the narrative that follows are some of the events that gave Snyder's warnings (and my own forebodings) new relevance. The somber meditations they inspired are my own. We are all the product of our individual experiences, and we tend to judge a macro world through the micro lens of our own perceptions, phobias, and longings.

Much can be blamed on the evils perpetrated by fictitious "communists" in the name of an imaginary and unworkable system of governance, including the rising appeal of totalitarianism in America.

*"To judge from the notions expounded by theologians,
one must conclude that God created most men simply
with a view to crowding hell."* —**Marquis de Sade (1740-1814)**

TRUMPISM AND MASS LUNACY—Nature, certainly, plays a part in sculpting humans, at least biologically. But nurture—that is, the milieu in which we evolve (and to which we unconsciously cling because the herding instinct is stronger than the eccentricity of apostasy)—has at least as much influence on how *"groupthink"* can transform individuals into robotized, narrow-minded conformists. History and enforced traditions have had a profound influence in shaping the America I discovered in 1956. I fault, in part, the Second Amendment, a misguided and hastily scripted addendum ratified in 1791 to allow the maintenance of *"a well-regulated Militia,"* but which was never intended to legalize individual arms-bearing rights. We have seen the quasi-erotic obsession that Americans have for their guns, not to mention their eagerness to use them. I also blame a mindset encoded by external stimuli that predisposes certain people to pick and choose the constitutional concepts and mandates they are willing to embrace, and those they fiercely believe they are entitled to disregard.

It was no surprise, viewed from a European perspective, the only one that offers me the luxury of critical comparison, that what I learned in high school ... laconic references to the near-extermination of indigenous peoples as slavery fueled America's economy; the commandeering of Hawaii, the Philippines, and Puerto Rico; the environmental and health damage caused by dozens of nuclear tests carried out in the 1940s and '50s in the Pacific, including a huge thermonuclear blast on Bikini Atoll; the death of at least 250.000 Japanese in Hiroshima and Nagasaki ... led me to view America as a nation of hot-headed brawlers.

What I discovered shortly after I arrived — *"White"* and *"Colored"* lunch counters, segregated toilets, drinking fountains, hotels, public transport, and schools, a contempt, if not open hostility toward Blacks, and the renaissance of the KKK—would fill me with dismay, fear, and revulsion, feelings I harbor to this day toward a segment of America that yearns for the "good old days." And I keep arguing that America's "heartland," shocked to its core by the nomination, election, and reelection of the first Black man made the incarnation and allure of a White supremacist despot named Donald J. Trump inevitable.

◆

Five weeks before the 2020 election, the first televised debate between Trump and Joe Biden highlighted all the concerns that arose over the past four years about the fragile state of democracy in the U.S. The most striking moments of this chaotic and brutal confrontation between the two septuagenarians were not Joe Biden's sighs of exasperation as a vulgar, pugnacious Trump kept interrupting him and whom he called a "clown." What will be remembered from Trump's tirades was his warning that the November 3 election *"will not end well."* It didn't, not for him, not for America.

Trump cast doubt on the validity of the presidential election and mail-in ballots expected in large numbers because of the Covid-19 pandemic. While Joe Biden pledged to respect the voters' will, Trump petulantly refused, should he lose, to concede defeat and to call on his fans to calm down if the results were not in his favor.

Trump's ambiguity over the conduct of the election was just as disturbing as his refusal to expressly condemn the violence of white supremacists, when he was urged to do so by the journalist leading the debate—not without difficulty. Trump would later instruct a far-right group, the Proud Boys, to *"stand back"* and urge them to *"stand ready."*

Such a repudiation of civism on the part of a U.S. president left us stunned. On the form, Trump's belligerence and rowdiness during this 90-minute verbal skirmish did not surprise those who have followed him since his first election campaign: He led the debate as he tweets — with an avalanche of invectives, self-glorification, accusations, and veiled threats. Democrats seemed offended, but the president's supporters lauded his militancy. It is this base that he is attempting to remobilize in advance of the 2024 elections.

On the substance, Trump's nonchalance over the electoral process, in tandem with his attacks on public services during his first term, must be sobering. Four years of Trumpism have significantly weakened one of the world's largest democracies. It's a lesson for all of us.

Highly anticipated abroad, the Trump-Biden face-off drew attention to the year 2020 — challenging for the world but especially painful for the U.S.: It began with a disastrous impeachment trial of the president and continued with urban violence echoing, in the midst of the pandemic, the growing polarization of American society. Two more debates were scheduled before the November 3rd election. In view of the sad spectacle offered by the first, several commentators wondered whether it might be appropriate to stop right there. It was right, in fact, to ask as they did how democracy would gain from yet another televised verbal duel.

◆

Meanwhile, the pandemic was causing an atmosphere of unease, uncertainty, confusion, suspicion, followed by intermittent acts of rebellion against masks and social distancing, and triggering unspeakable bursts of violence. There was a fear of riots and massive civil unrest whichever way the November 2020 presidential elections might turn out. Trump was even toying with the idea of postponing or suspending the elections *"because of Covid-19."* And he was discouraging voting by mail. I toyed with the idea that only some hideous miscegenation—stray DNA from history's fiends—Nero, Caligula, Hitler, Mussolini, Stalin, Mao, Ceausescu, Saddam Hussain, Idi Amin, and the Kim dynasty—could have spawned a villain like Trump.

I then wondered what psychological harm a *"new normal"* of long-term self-isolation would have on man's fragile psyche as scientists and health officials gingerly warned that the coronavirus will be with us for a long time to come … giving Mother Nature some respite but dooming humans to madness and premature death. I am talking about the nature of Nature. It is indeed neutral, impersonal. indifferent. Anger is a form of temporary madness fine-tuned by humans to its highest level of psychosis. Animals don't feel hatred. Wolves are not cruel; cruelty requires premeditation. Wolves behave as they were programmed by Nature. A lamb is not gentle; its calm, submissive demeanor is inscribed in its genes. Next time you watch a nature show, note the expression of a lion or tiger pursuing a gazelle. There isn't a scintilla of hatred or rage in their eyes. They are self-possessed, focused. They need to eat. In contrast, think of the hatred and murderous look in the eyes of the lunatics who stormed the Capitol on orders from their president.

The role of nature is self-perpetuation—from the bacterium to the butterfly to the whale to the elephant to the "naked ape." It does not distinguish between rich and poor, illiterate, and learned, imbecile and genius, Jew or Gentile, Democrat or Republican. It endows life and cuts it short on its own terms.

♦

Yes, it is fashionable to despise intelligent, educated people. They are hard to control, they can't be sold all sorts of junk. They upset the status quo. And so, over the last 50 years our insane society has groomed a new breed, a Homo sapiens look-alike, but with diminished gray matter. Movies often portray evil characters who are very intelligent, suggesting a correlation between intelligence and evil. Intelligence is hence seen as a threat, while a perfectly socialized idiot is a pillar of society.

Florida governor Ron DeSantis (like his counterparts in Texas and other flaming red states) is not a Malthusian theoretician. He is not an intellectual. He is not a scholar. Groomed, later scorned by Trump and inching his way to the presidency, he is a callous pragmatist devoid of moral principles. A right-wing extremist, he is insensitive to human suffering. His sole aim is to feed his political base of largely ignorant, uneducated white supremacists by spreading lies about the pandemic, masks, vaccination, and the "left's" plot to seize their precious guns. He angrily rejects the notion that the Earth's ecosystem is on the verge of collapse, or that human activity is in any way responsible for the violent atmospheric anomalies overwhelming the planet. Nor does he lose sleep comparing the calculus of deaths by the coronavirus versus crop failures and global food shortages. He does not have the mental capacity (or the heart) to see the horror of an end-all scenario. Would he act differently if he contracted the virus or lost a family member to it? Would he take the pandemic more seriously if he knew what it's like to die a Covid-19 death after having been fed high-doses of oxygen, while on ventilators, lung-bypass machines, blood thinners to prevent clots that attack organs and cause great pain, and steroids to reduce inflammation in the lungs? In advanced stages, the sickest patients at least have the mercy of being sedated. All he cares about is his career. He is such a power-hungry scoundrel that he threatened to withhold state funds from any school that encourages mask-wearing. And he is itching to create a Vatican-

44

style *Index of Prohibited Books* (abolished in 1966 by Pope Paul VI) to protect schoolchildren from heretical works.

The problem is not lockdowns, masks, social distancing, and frequent handwashing. The problem is people who are encouraged to think they are impervious to disease, who defy common sense and flout proven countermeasures. There is little doubt that if everyone heeded science instead of demented conspiracy theories, herd immunity would follow and the coronavirus—whose only raison d'être is to replicate—would retreat and disappear. But people are impatient and selfish. Every time there's been a relaxation a deadly surge occurred. We're dealing with a silent, invisible, tasteless, odorless monster that preys on vulnerable people. It is not going away any time soon.

The unspoken tragedy of this whole Covid experience has been the loss of humanity toward life. We used to have the ability to be with our loved ones when they were dying. Now people are dying alone, like animals in a jungle. Rationalizing other people's deaths, whether from disease or environmental disaster while enjoying our own lives, is unjust in the extreme. Justifying this injustice by reducing the problem to esoteric statistics is the height of cynicism.

> *"If you do not take an interest in politics, you are doomed to live under the rule of morons."*
> **—Plato (428-348 BCE)**

THE KEYS TO THE KINGDOM—Trump is not the first American to have set his sights on Greenland, the world's largest non-continental and least inhabited island. Although Harry Truman dodged questions about his pursuit of dominance in the region, the U.S. had tried to buy Greenland in 1867, then again in 1946. Trump's interest in the island speaks to its military and research potential. The territory is home to Thule Air Base, the U.S. military's northernmost base, located about 750 miles above the Arctic Circle and built in 1951. The radar and listening post features a Ballistic Missile Early Warning System that can warn of incoming intercontinental warheads and reaches thousands of miles into Russian territory. On the sordid side of things Trump might have been eyeing cheap real estate to erect a hotel, a casino, or, as the earth is now boiling and parts of Greenland are melting, a summer White House.

♦

Expansionism, a hallmark of U.S. foreign policy, has eyed other tempting targets. According to journalist/author Molly Caldwell Crosby, Cuba had long been considered a piece of prime real estate for expanding America's borders:

> *"At least four presidents had attempted to buy it. John Quincy Adams had called it a natural appendage to North America, and Thomas Jefferson had believed it to be 'the most interesting addition which could ever be made to our system of states.' Before the Civil War, the South hoped to annex Cuba as a slave state; after the Civil War, the North looked to it as a source of raw materials. The latest proponents, including Theodore Roosevelt, Henry Cabot Lodge, and Henry Adams ... considered Cuba 'part of our great manifest destiny.' It seemed clear that America had not only a right but a*

duty, bolstered by a growing navy, to enlighten others and protect [U.S.] interests in the western hemisphere. Cuba was the new frontier."

When Senator Bernie Sanders, casually but justifiably praised Fidel Castro's literacy initiatives, Trump, whose orgasmic worship of scoundrels (Russia's Vladimir Putin, Hungary's Viktor Orban, Turkey's Recep Tayyip Erdogan, Brazil's Jair Bolsonaro, and North Korea's Kim Jung Un, with whom he exchanged "love letters,") casts serious doubt on his morals, if not sanity, pounced on the Vermont lawmaker, accusing him of deifying a dictator and ... you guessed, flirting with "communism."

Whoa! President Fulgencio Batista (1901-1973), the man Castro unseated, was a dictator under whose governance unspeakable brutalities were committed against the Cuban people. Batista, *"Our Man in Cuba,"* suspended the 1940 Constitution and revoked most political liberties, including the right to strike.[2] He then aligned with the wealthiest landowners who operated the largest sugar plantations and presided over a stagnating economy that widened the gap between Cuba's rich

---

[2] Fascist dictator Francisco Franco was "Our Man in Spain." Shah Reza Pahlavi, who ordered the widespread torture and imprisonment of political dissidents, was "Our Man in Iran." Trained in the U.S., Gen. Augusto Pinochet, responsible for the murder/disappearance of more than 4,000 civilians, was "Our Man in in Chile." Papa Doc Francois Duvalier, a despot who ruled by fear, was "Our Man in Haiti." While useful as a foe of Iran, Saddam Hussein was "Our Man in in Baghdad." Embezzler and human rights violator, President Ferdinand Marcos, was "Our Man in the Philippines." Strongman Rafael Trujillo, whose state terrorism oversaw the massacre of between 12,000 and 30,000 Haitians in the infamous Parsley Massacre, was "Our man in the Dominican Republic." Manuel Noriega, a drug trafficker, was "Our Man in Panama." And while he fought the Russians, Usama bin Laden was "Our man in Afghanistan." All had longstanding ties to US intelligence agencies, including the CIA.

and poor. Eventually, most of the sugar industry was in U.S. hands and foreigners owned 70 percent of Cuba's arable land.

Batista's repressive government then began to profit from the exploitation of Cuba's commercial interests by negotiating lucrative relationships with both States-side organized crime families, which controlled the drug, gambling, and prostitution rackets in Havana, and with large U.S.-based multinational companies that were awarded profitable contracts. To quell the growing discontent among the populace—displayed through frequent student riots and demonstrations—Batista established tighter censorship of the media, while also utilizing his Bureau for the Repression of Communist Activities (secret police) to carry out wide-scale violence, torture, and public executions.

The long-awaited and since rescinded rapprochement between Cuba and the U.S. had been heartily applauded. Friendship and cooperation are always preferable to enmity, isolation, and distrust, especially in an epoch of worldwide turmoil and volatility. Should things improve with Trump out of the White House, I expressed the hope that the good people of Cuba would confine their relations with the U.S. to those trade and cultural transactions that are of distinct benefit to Cubans, which do not compromise the sovereignty of their nation, and that do not imperil the hard-fought Revolution. Cubans old enough to look back to the dark days of the Batista dictatorship will remember that Cuba, at the time, was a Mafia-controlled political stronghold and America's offshore whorehouse. It would be a great tragedy if normalization of relations between the two nations resulted in the economic buyout of Cuba by America's capitalist interests ... and organized crime syndicates. Such takeover would inevitably bring back the corruptive influences and misdeeds that precipitated the downfall of Cuba's economy in the 1950s. While I cannot hide my displeasure at some of Cuba's Stalin-style inequities and aberrations, I salute its brave and forbearing citizens.

♦

Strongmen rule by fear, complicity, and intimidation. [Trump's] *"personal qualities and talents,"* writes New York University history professor Ruth Ben-Ghiat,

> *"... proved ideal in corrupting and subjugating the GOP. He is not just a highly skilled propagandist, but also the embodiment of the man who gets away with everything – fraud, tax evasion, and sexual assault, to mention only his publicly known portfolio of criminal allegations."*

A corruption expert, widely published journalist, Casey Michel observes that Trump is the first western leader to emerge from *"the kleptocratic services industry"* via a real estate business that was long suspected of laundering money for oligarchs and mafiosi.

Trump is no intellectual, but I grant him the shrewdness and manipulative genius of an unhinged con man, the astuteness of a power-crazed predator who views everybody as a potential prey (or source of profit). The man is dangerous, and yet his reckless rhetoric keeps luring and infecting a sizeable segment of America's constituency. There were several narrow openings of hope in an otherwise very cloudy political sky: He kept making one mistake after another, telling lie after lie, threatening his adversaries, preening his precious ego, and yet his popularity did not decline sufficiently or fast enough to precipitate his ouster or prophesy a defeat in the 2020 election.

Nothing short of a miracle, I thought at the time, would help unseat him. If he loses, I predicted, he will claim the election was rigged and his gun-happy disciples are dumb enough, vicious enough, bigoted enough to believe him and engage in massive retributive acts of violence. My predictions came true on January 6, 2021. It was bad enough that Trump was at the helm. But what to do with the millions who worship him, who quote him, who emulate him ... and those in Congress who profit from their unholy allegiance to a man who doesn't care whether they live or die? I would not be surprised to learn that officials had compiled intelligence warning that white supremacists and other extremists were likely to assemble in Washington and storm the Capitol, and that future disruptions were likely. After all, hadn't a weekend of rage, hatred, violence, and death taken place four years earlier when white supremacists wielding semiautomatic rifles and pistols converged on Charlottesville, Virginia, flanked by self-styled militia members, all chanting, *"Jews will not replace us"*? Hadn't a neo-Nazi rammed his car into a crowd, killing 32-year-old counter-protester Heather Heyer and injuring at least 19 others? And hadn't I rationalized these events by gloating over British, Canadian, and US university studies which concluded that people with a low IQ are drawn to socially conservative ideologies, because they *"tend to offer structure and order,"* and that such ideologies can contribute to prejudice and violence?

♦

Trump had become both the symbol and incarnation of America's diseased psyche. Should he vanish, a replica, I was convinced, would emerge from the Right's cloning factories, and take center stage. America was ripe for a fascist takeover and presidential aspirants, one wackier, more blinkered, and inept than the other would soon claim the nation's keys to the newly crowned totalitarian kingdom of God and his ever-multiplying creation.

I remember asking myself: Is Trump a deflection, a *"Trump-l'oeil"*? Is something sinister brewing behind the scenes, whose origins and aims will not be revealed until it's too late? No matter what happens, I was forced to admit, America will never be the same. The evil that Trump has done will live after him. Now empowered, his followers can be expected to poison whatever is left of the future … and spawn another swindler/megalomaniac who will fan the embers of hatred for fun and profit.

> *"We don't inherit the earth from our ancestors,*
> *we borrow it from our children."*
> **—Native American proverb**

THE WORLD AS WE KNEW IT—It's snowing in British Columbia. Typhoons batter the western Pacific. Killer tornadoes flatten hundreds of square miles of human habitat. Barreling toward the northwest, blinding snowstorms entomb several states, while glaciers in Greenland, the snows of the Kilimanjaro and the Himalayan peaks melt at an unprecedented rate, threatening the water supply of some 250 million of people in Asia.

Denying (or ignoring) the aftershocks of global warming is not a partisan affair. Like death and taxes, it will affect everyone, conservative and liberal, rich, and poor, learned and illiterate, sick and robust, young, and old. Beach erosion, the result of flooding caused by melting polar ice and cataclysmic downpours will continue to chew up increasingly larger chunks of coastal regions, including Bangladesh and low-lying Pacific islands (Tuvalu, Kiribati, Palau, the Solomons, Maldives, and Seychelles). Parts of Vietnam, Japan, Ireland, and Holland are now underwater. Much of Venice may soon become permanently submerged. After suffering the second-worst flood in its history in November 2019, the "Queen of the Adriatic" was inundated by four more exceptionally high tides in six weeks, shocking Venetians and triggering fears about the catastrophic impact of climate change.

Miami is struggling with serious swamping related to sea-level rise—even when there is no precipitation. And when it rains, as it does often torrentially, many of the Magic City's streets turn into rivers. The ground under the cities of south Florida is porous limestone, which means water rises through it, compromising subterranean foundations and causing some buildings to collapse.[3]

The state is spending millions on flood-control measures, installing pumps, raising roads, and restoring wetlands. Seaside cities around the world, among them New York, face similar threats. As a result, millions of people will be displaced, adding to the already unstoppable exodus of refugees who are fleeing dysfunctional regimes, political upheavals, droughts, crop failures, human rights abuses, famine, crime, gang violence, and sectarian strife. It is the fate of coastal cities that was on the minds of climatologists and global leaders meeting in Glasgow, Scotland, at a U.N. climate conference that began in October 2021. Nations attending the meeting adopted a range of agreed initiatives, including strengthened efforts to build resilience to climate change, to curb greenhouse gas emissions and to provide the necessary finance for both. Nations also reaffirmed their duty to fulfill the pledge of providing $100 billion annually from developed to developing countries. And they collectively agreed to work to reduce the gap between existing emission reduction plans and what is required to reduce emissions, so that the rise in the global average temperature can be limited to 1.5 degrees centigrade. For the first time, nations are called upon to phase down unabated coal power and inefficient subsidies for fossil fuels.

◆

---

[3] On June 24, 2021, the 20-year-old Champlain Towers South, a 12-story beachfront "luxury" condominium in the Miami suburb of Surfside, collapsed. Ninety-eight people died. Long-term degradation of reinforced concrete structural support in the basement-level parking garage due to water penetration and corrosion of the reinforcing steel are blamed for the collapse. Could it have been shoddy construction? The Pont Neuf, Paris's oldest bridge is more than 400 years old. It's still standing. So is my alma mater, the Sorbonne, built in 1253.

Those who can afford to live on a beachfront estate are probably rich enough to find a drier spot by absconding to higher ground on their private jet or ocean-going yacht. The punchline no one seems to get is that it's the not-so-rich and millions of dirt-poor coastal populations who risk drowning in all-consuming floods of angry surf and toxic sludge.

Reflecting on a society doomed to fight desperately for survival on a dying planet, Umair Haque, a columnist for the Harvard Business Review asks:

> *"And yet one of the great challenges in the grim dystopia we face is as invisible as it is demanding. Can our empathy survive? What about decency, courage, strength, grace, generosity, humility? Can our consciousness — battered and bruised — withstand the end of the world as we know it?"*

Meditations about mankind's trials and tribulations, musings about man's virtues or lack thereof, are irrational: We already know the answer. What we are induced, in some cases forced, to believe (we are born innocent, unknowing, and prejudice-free) inevitably colors our perception of our microcosm by fashioning a "reality" that is often worlds away from observable, verifiable actuality. Simply put, we believe what we want to believe or, in extremis, what we are told to believe—"facts" be damned. As author Robert Heinlein famously said, *"Man is a rationalizing animal, not a rational one."*

Some of us live in the present. Others are obsessed with the future. Uncertainty, life's unpredictability, are a constant source of anxiety. Others yet cling to a past they cannot replicate. To lessen the stress, they latch on to certain storylines that harmonize with their core beliefs, not with the truth. If it sounds plausible, it must be true. Humans cannot perceive reality directly but only through a multitude of myths, religious and political. These myths are so common and so widespread that a typical human gets entangled in them and no longer perceives objective reality. It's as if our thinking apparatus is so seriously underdeveloped or damaged that we cannot think coherently for extended periods of time.

We hear it said, often with censorious annoyance *"I'm entitled to my opinions."* Yes, but an opinion is not a fact. Unless you're Aquinas or Aristotle, Socrates or Sartre, Spinoza or Camus, your opinions are likely mundane if not trivial. Even my polarizing takes on the human condition can easily be invalidated by a louder, more menacing voice. We generally adopt those positions that most closely harmonize with the drummed-in beliefs and prejudices of our parents, teachers, "spiritual" guides, and favorite shock-jock. We cling to them because independent and critical thinking requires an enormous capital of intellectual latitude and moral courage, not to mention a gray matter uncontaminated by immovable beliefs. Worse, we shamelessly peddle them while being convinced of our own deductive faculties. The great tragedy is that few of us care about the lies that opinions might conceal. They are the dungeons in which we lock ourselves by feigning a clear conscience — very often the result of a bad memory. Most of our beliefs are built on a vast scaffolding of dogmas, doctrines, preconceptions, and chimeras often advanced by someone else. And yet we believe that they are the result of our own ruminations because they protect us from what we fear most — the truth.

Everybody has opinions. Naïve or wacky, they are easily deconstructed and dismissed. Inflexible or toxic, they blind us, inflate us with arrogance. Taken to the extreme, they drive us mad. Opining from emotion does the truth a disservice. It just makes us feel better about ourselves because, heavens forbid, we should be wrong about anything that comes out unreflexively out of our mouths. And yet, they're the devices with which the truth is often sacrificed. Without them there would be nothing to talk about.

W. E. Gutman

> "God created war so that Americans
> would learn geography."
> — **Mark Twain (1835-1910)**

LET US PREY—In the age of extinction, we are told, only love remains. Are we capable of loving indiscriminately? Or do we reserve our affection and loyalty for those closest to us? We hear love being preached in houses of worship, these temples of mendacity where the fears and obsessions and hopes and chimeras that haunt us are staged to induce jubilant hysteria or mournful self-contemplation. And we know that when the swaying, trembling outstretched arms that reach skyward come down, when the last amen and the final breathless hallelujahs have been uttered, when feverish eyes that glimpsed the face of "God" and sought salvation in a trance-like moment of ecstasy have reopened, the faithful, these pious souls, these model citizens, their ears still ringing from some exalted homily or sacred hymn, will reconnect with the profane world from which they come and the guzzling, the fornicating, the indiscriminate breeding, the gossiping, the hatred, the lying, the killing will resume.

I am not without empathy, but the feeling is abstract, not visceral. I'd be a hypocrite if I claimed that I can love anyone beyond the people in my life. And I'm not even sure it's love. Age, I discover, has spawned a persistent but guiltless repugnance to all manners of distractions and irritants: Noise; traffic; slow drivers; homicidal/suicidal drivers; people who talk too much; people who talk with their hands; busybodies and know-it-alls; chauvinists and flag-waivers; selfie-takers; soccer moms; mystics and religious zealots; cheerleaders and motivational speakers; military parades; the Second Amendment; the Electoral College; spelling bees; televangelists; hog-calling contests; Tupperware parties; rodeos; American "football" and rugby (violence and mayhem for the sake of violence and mayhem); wrestling (the vulgar, violent simulation of violence); NASCAR (noise and violence on wheels); hunting and bullfighting; people who start a sentence with *"So"* when nothing preceding it suggests consequence or disclosure; teens who insert "like" six times in a seven-word sentence; old women who dress like Shirley Temple and paint their upper lip crimson red; smart phones and the boors who use them in public. However irrational or insensitive these aversions might be, I shall not part with them. They enliven my existence.

Love? My friend Kulbir, a devout Sikh, says that the Gurus' wisdom can help turn ordinary humans into kind and virtuous beings. I know him to be a righteous man. Having perused the *Guru Granth Sahib*, Sikhism's sacred scriptures, I recognize in Kulbir the incarnation and emissary of teachings that promote and practice equality among all races irrespective of caste, religion, color, status, age, or gender, that respect positive ideals like truth, empathy, contentment, humility, and love, and that decry the inner evils of lust, anger, greed, material attachment, and ego. I asked Kulbir the question that "Yevgeny" had once asked me: Do humans have *"value."* He found the question both absurd and offensive. Kulbir put his faith in the ferryman and crossed the river unscathed. He found his *"place."* I'm still struggling to keep afloat in its raging current.

◆

Religious faith is taught, imprinted, sometimes even beaten into children born with a clean slate and devoid of fear and preconceptions. I don't believe in a *"God"* gene (the reductionist theory that human spirituality is influenced by heredity and that a specific gene predisposes humans towards spiritual or mystic experiences). Taken to extremes, religion acquires all the characteristics of full-blown psychosis.

About 85 percent of humans believe in a pantheon of *"gods."* The most popular is an invisible, deaf, mute (but omnipotent) spirit inhabiting the nether regions of the cosmos and ready to consign you for the slightest peccadillo to the infernal depths of Gehenna (but he loves you!). Others are carved out of wood, sculpted out of granite, or molded from clay. Others yet are unseen but said to be perched on the highest mountains, inhabiting the deepest lakes, and haunting the most impenetrable forests. Many people also believe that once they trash this planet and die, they will be transported to a *"better place"* which they will likely proceed to destroy. Religion has been fostering apocalypse as a logical end of its world model and earthly existence, and generations have been raised to invoke it, not to prevent it. Would *"God"* be willing to create another world for us if we fail to save this one? He'd be a fool if he did.

If we can blame one institution for our mental decrepitude and looming demise it's not the banks, corporations, gun merchants, or crooked politicians. It's religion. Whereas enlightenment is a state of mental illumination that transcends dogma and rigid ideas, religion is the single greatest obstacle to the kind of tolerance and open-mindedness that the enlightened radiate. Religion is divisive and exclusionary, and a major source of conflict. More blood has been shed in its name than any other cause.

There are about 150 recognized religions, each insisting it has a direct Hypertext Transfer Protocol link to God. If that's not against the laws of physics ... I don't know what is. But then again, there is nothing logical about religion ... which is why illogical humans still believe in fairy tales — the literary kind and their politicized variants. Everywhere, all I see is greed, selfishness, indifference, hypocrisy, corruption, and folly.

I've known pious people of every faith. Underneath the ecstasy, the jubilation, and the hallelujahs lurk dark fears and self-doubts and unanswered prayers that the faithful awkwardly attribute to *"God's strange and mysterious ways."* Most corrosive is the subconscious fear of lapsing convictions, an-ever present state of mind that sends the faithful to extremes of religiosity — ritualistic, mechanical, frenzied. Such people are to be pitied because that's all they have. What appears to be euphoria is in fact repressed anxiety.

I have also known people who never go to church but quietly, anonymously worship "God" (or some undefinable "Grand Architect of the Universe") in the temple of their own mind. For others, religion without histrionics is meaningless. The Mass and frenzied revivalist rituals are stirring reminders of the grandiose power of staged mysticism. It's free entertainment.

For two thousand years we have been waiting for the end of the world and the Second Landing. It did not happen. The navigator got drunk, plotted the wrong course, got lost, and slammed the vessel into a razor-sharp shallow reef. Religion asserts that a talking monkey has transcendental worth in the Universe. While a talking monkey is an interesting phenomenon — though not as innocent or deserving of mercy as the great apes that preceded him — his worth has been seriously overestimated. He is dangerous enough in the buff. Armed with *"God"* he becomes criminally insane. *"Love thy neighbor"*? Very noble advice when the neighbor is one of *"us."* Otherwise, it's rubbish. It is much easier to hate than to love. History proves it.

◆

America has a long tradition of religious fundamentalism and fanaticism. The first settlers believed in witches and brought them to trial. To force a confession of heresy and witchcraft, two young men in Salem were trussed at their necks and heels until blood oozed from their noses. A poor immigrant in Boston, speaking only Irish and saying her simple prayers in Latin, was hanged as a witch because she couldn't recite the Lord's Prayer in English. We now know how the "Holy" Inquisition, which endured well into the early 19th century, was involved in the institutionalization of witchcraft and how it was able to create witchcraft where it did not exist by means of torture, shrewd interrogation techniques, and psychological pressure. The last person to be executed by the Inquisition was Cayetano Ripoll, a Spanish schoolmaster hanged for heresy in 1826. The fears such methods inspired were reinforced by fiery Sunday and feast-day sermons. Didn't the book of Apocalypse predict that the coming of the Antichrist would be heralded by great swarms of heretics and witches? There once was a law in Massachusetts that called for unmarried couples who lived together to be taken to the gallows, made to stand there for an hour with a rope around their necks and receive thirty-nine lashes. The 1784 decree, which prohibited couples from *"lasciviously associating and cohabitating without the benefit of marriage,"* lived in the law books until its repeal by then Governor Michael S. Dukakis in April 1987. That would not prevent the selectman of the town of Sharon, a Boston suburb., from citing the abolished blue law against Officer Linda F. Farris, 36, the first woman on the Sharon police force and Officer Lawrence Phaneuf, 39, with whom Farris was living. In an obscene display of fake puritanism and misogyny, Farris was dismissed from the force and Phaneuf was demoted. The record of witchcraft is horrible and brutal. The filthiest passions masqueraded under the cover of religion, and man's intellect was subverted to condone bestialities that even Swift's Yahoos would have blushed to commit.

Settlers were also fond of massacring *"Injuns"* in the Lord's name. Small towns and rural areas remain to this day bastions of fanatical religiosity. I once attended (as an uninvolved spectator...) an evangelical Christian *"revival,"* a free-for-all affair during which people faint, jump up and down like demented macaques, talk in *"tongues,"* weep uncontrollably, handle deadly snakes, and throw themselves into the arms of the *"pastor"* — generally a clever con man who drives home to his multi-million-dollar mansion in his Maserati, both the earthly rewards his flock's blessed largesse enables him to enjoy. After all, money is good, he tells his flock.

> *"Regardless of what you may have been taught, God wants you to be rich so that you may enjoy the good things money can buy, and because it is divinely right for you to be rich."*

Belief in witchcraft, while less widespread than five centuries ago, is still alive today. Witch hunts, as did those set off by Senator Joe McCarthy's hysterical rants, continue to target "communists," atheists, purveyors of *"fake news,"* and *"enemies of the people."*

♦

I cried the other day when I heard that a poacher in Africa had been killed by an elephant he had wounded and was then devoured by a lion. I cried for the elephant, cheered for the lion. Justice triumphed. Yet deep down inside, I also recognized in me the distant, formless longing to see peace prevail in a world that has learned, at long last, not to hate. It's a yearning that has no future. I shall keep it entombed.

*"If you want to tell people the truth,
make them laugh, or else they will kill you."*
—**George Bernard Shaw (1856-1950)**

A DEPLORABLE TRUTH—We'd been warned. During her 2016 presidential campaign, Hillary Clinton cautioned America that Donald Trump and his *"basket of deplorables,"* the salt of America's earth—racist, sexist, homophobic, xenophobic, Islamophobic, pious Christians—threatened democracy. This was no idle prophecy but a statement of fact that cost her the election. In politics, the truth is not a marketable commodity. Journalists get killed for exhuming it.

Clinton's portrayal of the Neanderthals who worship Trump and defiled the Capitol was also a clarion call about the backsliding politics and hostile values that Trump's followers still embrace—white supremacy, anti-intellectualism, a love of guns, a penchant for violence, a predisposition toward despotism, and a contagious malady that afflicts deplorables: pride of ignorance, better defined as the arrogant disdain of knowledge, which everyone knows is the devil's work.

Transforming a democracy into a dictatorship is a process, not a spontaneous event. Hillary Clinton had been eerily perceptive. During an interview in 1998 she had famously warned of a *"vast right-wing conspiracy"* that sought to destroy her husband's presidency. Clinton revisited that warning in 2016 during a televised town hall meeting in New Hampshire:

"At this point it's probably not correct to say it's a conspiracy because it's out in the open. There is no doubt about who the players are and what they're trying to achieve. [The multibillionaires] want to control our country. They want to rig the economy so they can get richer and richer. They salve their consciences by giving money to philanthropy but make no mistake,

they want to destroy unions, they want to go after any economic interest they don't believe they can control."

Addressing America's democracy crisis and the Republican threats to human and civil rights. Clinton added,

"There is a plot against the country by people who truly want to turn the clock back. They believe that the progress we've made on all kinds of civil rights and human rights, the cultural changes that have taken place, are so deeply threatening that they want to stage a coup."

Hillary Clinton envisioned and described what would happen if Trump and his cronies took over. She was right on all counts about the all-too-real *"vast right-wing conspiracy"* that undermines human rights, human dignity, social democracy, and freedom.

Writing in *Caste: The Origins of Our Discontent*, bestselling author, Isabel Wilkerson, reminded us that,

"... For the first time in history, a woman was running as a major party candidate for president of the United States. A household name, the candidate was a non-nonsense national figure overqualified by some estimates. Conventional and measured if uninspiring to her detractors, with a form grasp of any policy or crisis that she might be called upon to address. Her opponent was an impetuous billionaire, a reality television star prone to insulting most anyone unlike himself, who had never held public office and who pundits believed had no chance of winning his party's primaries much less the presidency. Before the campaign was over, the male candidate would stalk the female candidate from behind during a debate seen all over the world. He would boast of grabbing women by their genitals, mock the disabled, incite violence against the press and against those who disagreed with him."

Or as chess grandmaster and Russian political activist, Gary Kasparov, once remarked,

"The point of disinformation is not just to get people to accept a lie. It is to annihilate truth and to exhaust people's defense of the truth."

Pride of ignorance is the suit of armor of those who have no use for knowledge and the truth.

> *"The more a society drifts from truth,*
> *the more it will hate those who speak it."*
> **—George Orwell (1903-1950)**

ON WRITING, HERESY, & APOCALYPSE—The prospect that what I write may not be read (or that I will be maligned) has never discouraged me from writing. No parallel intended, but Mozart, who died young and poor, did not compose in the hope of being heard any more than Van Gogh, who only sold one painting (to his brother) stopped painting because his work was unpopular or woefully unappreciated at the time. Nor did the hypnotic Franz Kafka, whose copious output he destined for the pyre (but was rescued by his friend Max Brod) ceased churning out one surreal allegory after another. They all kept creating because an inner urge compelled them to do so. Their "motivation" was the journey, not the destination.

Writing is a path to self-revelation. It helps the writer think, clarify, and refine views and attitudes on a variety of subjects, reinforcing some, rejecting others that do not meet the test of time, credibility, logic, or impartiality. You learn a lot about yourself in the process. I wrote things twenty years ago that I regret writing and which I subsequently consigned to the scrap heap. I also penned hasty drafts that I had a chance to revise and polish twenty years later. My job ends when I type the last period at the end of the final paragraph. I don't care whether readers send me flowers or shoot poisoned arrows.

♦

I made a career of pissing people off by telling inconvenient truths in more than 600 newspaper and magazine articles, and fifteen books. Net result: Nothing has changed. About 99 percent of my audience kept silent. It is statistically possible that a few concurred with my views but found no compelling reason to say so publicly; others disagreed but kept their opinions to themselves. Others yet were mad as hell. I earned at least two death threats in the process. The rest agreed with my polemics and were brave enough to speak up or, incensed by my irreverence, drowned their ire in dark, simmering silence.

I had a lot of fun but made no money—which is the fate of writers, artists, composers, etc., who are victim not of their unrecognized genius but of the public's staggering shallowness, indifference, and pedestrian tastes. The poetry of dissidence and the science of apocalypse are distractions for which people have no stomach. You can't enjoy life when you're constantly bombarded with reminders of how little you know and with cues about your impending demise. It is the destiny of close-ended dystopias to be read as dark entertainment ... and forgotten.

One apocalyptic scenario that current events seem to hint at is the possibility of an instantaneous and unpreventable catastrophe that wipes out all life forms in a single event, perhaps cosmic in origin—say a supernova which has the capability of mass destruction and whose effects can be felt from thousands of light years away—or a nuclear holocaust. These are calamities I can live with. I cannot imagine enduring an apocalyptic "environment" (translation: slow, painful death)—a dearth of food and water, disease, the breakdown of civil order, lawlessness, vigilante justice, riots, looting, and mass murder. The prospect that a once fertile and bountiful planet, now a lifeless wasteland, will continue to spin around its axis, revolve around the sun and, after centuries if not millennia of ecological hibernation, will begin to spawn some primitive organisms is no consolation, especially to those who warned of such impending fate.

I recently dreamed—or was it my third eye validating instinct honed by experience—that the world was anticipating a nuclear conflagration.[4] Instead of panic, people were jubilant, festive. Instead of retreating into hardened bunkers, they flocked to the streets, gathered on balconies, terraces, and rooftops, their eyes fixed on some distant spot in space, joyfully awaiting the all-consuming flash and thermonuclear storm, ready to take their last breath before being pulverized. I stood there among them, unconcerned, a numbing euphoria coursing through my veins. I awoke briefly to assess the damage and went back to sleep. Time melts into an unending continuum of anxiety and boredom, impatience, and irritation. A new type of primal fear keeps us in its grip. The lotto wheel is spinning; no one knows where it will stop.

◆

Journalism is not a profession for *"the summer soldier or the sunshine patriot."*[5] It's a calling, a vocation, a mission that surpasses the exigencies of a job, a moral contract that journalists worthy of the name make with themselves and who know no other way to appeal to reason than by uncovering and imparting essential truths. We suffer from a kind of sublime curse that pushes us to reveal niggling truths and point a finger at those who want to bury them. It's a thankless task yet we spend a lifetime polishing an unyielding ashlar. Being misunderstood, even hated, is a kind of victory we must grant ourselves while acknowledging that nothing ever changes. The strange thrill sharpens our energy. It becomes the fuel that keeps us going.

◆

---

[4] The extra-sensory driving force that awakens the creative process; the ability to look deeply at some aspect of reality and discern underlying axiomatic truths.

[5] *The American Crisis*. Thomas Paine (1736-1809).

I spent twelve years in Central America (1994-2006), more precisely in the bowels of a beast that, under the tutelage of decaying, inept, arrogant dynastic regimes, not only refuses to evolve but marinates in a miasma of corruption, destitution, violence (street children and indigenous minorities are routinely harassed, often murdered by agents of the state) and despair. My reports and commentaries earned me, on two occasions (one in Guatemala, the other in Honduras) death threats so serious that I had to beat a hasty retreat, the latter in the middle of the night. I came back, ready to resume otherwise unwinnable battles.

◆

It's not always easy to tell crooks or outlaws from choir boys. What I learned about the CIA's role in Latin America, more specifically during my 12 years in the Isthmus, would make anyone's hair stand on end. The tragic irony is that the *"Company's"* dirty deeds—from narcotics trafficking to the funding of death squads that massacred thousands of peasants, to the "disappearance" of journalists, teachers, union organizers, liberal priests, to the purchase of small arms from Israel to equip local constabularies with weapons used to assassinate tribal leaders and homeless minors—are an open secret widely reported in the U.S. media and long since swept under the rug and forgotten.

◆

As a child in France, I remember witnessing the execution of ten elderly men in retaliation for the murder of a German officer who had been screwing the butcher's daughter. Devastating spectacle dulled by time. What shocked me even more, 50-plus years later, was the murder, in broad daylight in Tegucigalpa, of a young man who stole a piece of bread from an outdoor stall. The vendor quietly put the gun back in his pocket. No one intervened. No one protested. Armed with Israeli assault rifles, the police came, looked at the cadaver, and walked away. In some places, hunger is punishable by death.

The U.S. continues to maintain a discreet military presence in Honduras, a corrupt, inept failed state ruled (perhaps jointly) by about ten dynastic families who own newspapers, hotels, sweat shops, bus companies, telecommunication networks, electric, gas, and water utilities, and by organized crime cartels. The Soto Cano Air Base is partly operated by the U.S. which maintains an economic stranglehold on a nation that has never known democracy. Billeted in Columbus, Georgia, the U.S. Army School of the Americas continues to graduate soldiers and officers trained, not to protect their country from foreign enemies … but to keep their own people *"in place."*

Vietnam was another horror, another illegal, immoral, and unwinnable war that America waged in the name of "democracy." It's amazing how many people *"The Leader of the Free World"* has been willing to kill to maintain its political and economic preeminence.

Back from Central America, thoroughly nauseated by the corruption, the violence, the grotesque ineptitude and venality of successive regimes, each unwilling to clean up the mess they created, I set my sights on the United States. Those who understand me are silent. The others call me an apostate, a heretic, a traitor. Some go even so far as to accuse me of being a "communist." These absurd denunciations are sweet music to my ears. *Condemnant quod non intellegunt.*[6]

---

[6] They disparage what they do not understand.

*"The truth is more likely to have been discovered by
one man than by an entire nation."*
— **René Descartes (1596-1650)**

JOURNALISM AT THE CROSSROADS — They say that journalism is the first draft of history. Indelible images of the human drama are seized then frozen in time on the printed page and replayed on the airwaves. Delivered warts and all, facts should discourage revisionists from tampering with the truth. Alas, for many, fact has become calumny, reality a foe, truth heresy. For those whose only loyalty is to the truth, it's a lonely world. The price for such devotion is often steep and those who are willing to pay for it never lack enemies. Are some media hurtling down the rabbit hole of evasion, stonewalling, and conscious self-censorship? Who speaks for those who cannot speak freely?

To the enemies of truth, journalists make an appetizing quarry. If our exposés or commentaries are too graphic, irreverent, or too close for comfort, we're accused of needlessly giving readers palpitations. No matter what we report, we're sure to be reviled by someone along the way. Of course, readers are not a homogeneous lot. They come in sundry stripes and hues and biases. Mercifully, many seek to be informed. Many possess the intellectual elasticity to judge news reports and editorials on their own merits. It is to them that scrupulous journalists devote their reports and risk their lives with increasingly tragic consequences.

Countless readers, hasty or inattentive like disoriented butterflies, take things out of context and misconstrue. They see conspiracy in syntax. They scrutinize and dissect every utterance as if it concealed some subversive coded message. They can't see the sentence from the words. Some advocate expurgation. They are so jarred by the truth that they want it suppressed, obliterated, reduced to ashes ... along with the journalists who report it.

Not all journalists rush in where angels fear to tread. Some are daunted by the naked truth. Political correctness—the sacrifice of truth at the altar of hypocrisy—keeps readers and advertisers happy. Unlike open scandal, which peaks in an orgy of vitriol and rebuke, then dies, self-censorship (or dialectic pussyfooting) leaves a trail of speculations and a scent of putrefaction. It's bad enough when politicians hide behind a wall of secrecy and lies, it's worse when the media, the conscience of a free society, sheepishly corrupt their mission by colluding to keep the public in the fog of ignorance. It is the height of obscenity when politicians vilify the Fourth Estate or want it silenced.

Despite opinions to the contrary, journalists do not get paid to generate solutions for the problems we cite. Our job is to observe and report. Solutions can only be extracted from the problems themselves and from those who create them. What emerges from some readers' comments—generally in the cowardly shadow of anonymity—is the appalling suggestion that divulging verifiable facts is an act of disloyalty. A free, independent press is the bedrock of democracy, especially where democracy is being systematically eroded. Analytical criticism is not unpatriotic. It's a fundamental right, an obligation, and the manifestation of a nation's wisdom and social conscience. Silence is the real villain.

> *"People always talk about the public interest,*
> *but all they really care about*
> *is themselves and private property."*
> **—Utopia, Thomas More (1478-1535)**

1619: A YEAR TO REMEMBER—Suddenly, everybody is invoking the Constitution, some to awaken America's flaccid conscience by reaffirming its noblest ideals, others to justify their spurious claim that they have the right to reject them. For many, a compact's legitimacy must include the privilege to ignore, even defy it. On the eve of America's 246th anniversary as a nation, I look back at its infancy. On July 2nd, 1776, the Continental Congress voted to declare independence from the British monarch, King George III. The actual Declaration of Independence was signed two days later, on July 4th. The Declaration, authored principally by Thomas Jefferson, was a visionary document that set the country's white supremacist history and capitalist future in motion. In his original draft, Jefferson wrote:

> *"We hold these truths to be sacred & undeniable, that all men are created equal & independent, that from that equal creation they derive rights inherent & inalienable, among which are the preservation of life, & liberty, & the pursuit of happiness..."*

Further down in the document, after a long list of grievances, Jefferson added that King George was responsible for ...

> *"...waging cruel war against human nature itself, violating its most sacred rights of life & liberty in the persons of a distant people who never offended him, captivating & carrying them into slavery..."*

What! At the time, Britain had outlawed slavery. He signed into Law the abolition of the slave trade in 1807. Fact is that George was a good-natured, enlightened constitutional monarch, a man who was horrified by royalist tyranny, and who denounced it at every opportunity. He was so fond of the Magna Carta and English common law that he never considered trying to use extra-legal powers against the American Revolution until the first shots were fired at Lexington and Concord ... by the colonists.

Jefferson—ironically a slaveholder himself (and the father of several children with his enslaved mulatto concubine, Sally Hemings)—goes on and on in a similar vein, the most extended single idea of the declaration. But that passage was deleted from the final version by the Continental Congress ... and slavery, which would fester for another 250 years, ended up not being mentioned at all. That seemingly inconsequential decision, which ultimately drove the U.S. to civil war, has been conspicuously omitted from school history curricula as well.

◆

In Lincoln's Gettysburg address we find the phrase *"and dedicated to the proposition that all men are created equal."* By "all men" one must assume Lincoln included all of humanity. But a proposition is a statement or assertion that expresses a judgment or opinion. It's a recommendation, which, by inference and intent implies a certain degree of uncertainty relative to its merits or likelihood of universal acceptance. It's wishful thinking. When someone proposes, someone else disposes ... and not always to the proposer's satisfaction. Both Jefferson and Lincoln understood the tactical value of rhetorical flourish. But both were wrong or disingenuous: Men are not, never have been, never will be "created equal." That claim is a cruel hoax. We are born rich or poor, stupid, or smart, healthy, or prone to disease, creative or intellectually sterile. We are then further divided by social and cultural status, by the lies our parents tell us, the outlandish fictions peddled by our "spiritual leaders," by race, skin color, and tinted perceptions of the universe. And we lose all freedom and individuality when we seek (or are forced) to follow the flock because even the so-called "opportunities" to reach *equalhood* are asymmetrical.

◆

The view, recently revived, that the socio-economic and political character of what would become the United States was forged in August 1619, when the first slave ship landed at Point Comfort in the British colony of Virginia, and not on July 4, 1776, when the colonists declared independence from Britain, is something that many Americans find hard to swallow. But slavery is what fueled America's economy for 250 years and this monstrosity indeed began in August 1619 when 30 to 40 African men and women in shackles, weakened by disease and a long sea voyage, were sold and consigned to a life of unending toil, abuse, humiliation, and premature death. Out of the barbaric system of chattel slavery grew nearly everything that has truly made America exceptional and aberrant: its economic might, income inequality, its asymmetrical and prejudicial legal and electoral system, the inequities of its public health and education protocols, an astonishing penchant for violence, and the annoying pretense that it is a land of freedom and equality while endemic racial fears and hatreds continue to plague it to this day.

Predictably, serving red meat as bait to his political base two months before the presidential election, Donald Trump, America's Caligula, banned federal agencies from conducting race-sensitivity training related to "white privilege" and Critical Race Theory (CRT) which he claimed amounts to *"divisive, anti-patriotic propaganda."* This revisionist ploy follows a pattern by the former president of denigrating attempts to process or reckon with the country's fraught racial history. Moreover, the argument that CRT would imbue white students with a sense of guilt is as spurious as it is outlandish. Most white students are too busy taking selfies and engaging in moronic babble on social media to experience remorse for atrocities that they know nothing about because history textbooks continue to conceal or whitewash the truth.

The reasoning by opponents that if CRT does not address the notion that racism is innate across all cultures and that racism is a prerequisite to the institution of slavery everywhere, then it falls short of its goals, is a clear case of circular logic, artful equivocation. This argument fails to account for the fact that all colonizing nations eventually ditched their ill-gotten overseas possessions and publicly admitted (if not expiated) their sins. Since the fall of the Third Reich, Germany has bent over backward to redress its past by compensating Holocaust victims and their families and by enacting laws that severely punish the display of Nazi artefacts and the public utterance of anti-Semitic slurs. Smart people have at last concluded that free speech has it limits and consequences.

CRT addresses a uniquely American phenomenon, one that has endured for 250 years (plus another 150 years of Jim Crow laws and a lingering climate of intolerance). As such, CRT cannot be tasked to account for the egregious behavior of other nations. The mere fact that CRT critics argue that it is based on *"storytelling instead of evidence and reason"* — a slanderous lie — and that conservative U.S. lawmakers have sought to ban or restrict the instruction of CRT along with other anti-racist education in primary and secondary schools, is ample proof of its accuracy and relevance. Should Holocaust education be banned because it does not address other genocides? Should the mass murder of Native Americans be stricken from history books because, as some historians suggest, the victims of America's Conquista were neither peaceable nor harmless (translation: savages)?

Alas, people believe in lies and conspiracy theories because the truth is often too much to bear. They take refuge in a self-woven cocoon of ignorance and self-delusion. Nothing is more dangerous than simpletons who cling to opinions that are not their own (no opinion is original) because it spares them the effort (and risk) of thinking outside the box.

If one counts more than a million Native Americans massacred since the colonists arrived in North America, 250 years of slavery, segregation and persecution, 134 wars, the internment in concentration camps of some 120,000 Japanese men, women, and children (most of them U.S. citizens), the violent seizure of the Philippines, Hawaii, Cuba, Puerto Rico, and several Pacific islands, the murder by atom bomb of some 250,000 Japanese civilians in Hiroshima and Nagasaki, and the support of dictators in Latin America which resulted in the disappearance or assassination by CIA-funded death squads of thousands of labor leaders, journalists, progressive clergy, human rights advocates, and leftist politicians who had been freely elected (Guatemala, the Dominican Republic, Chile, etc.) ... one will quickly conclude that the U.S. is not substantially more virtuous than any other country. The only difference, maybe, is that the U.S. showed great resolve as it tried, by force, to sell democracy where it was neither understood nor wanted.

According to its detractors, Critical Race Theory is an academic framework that centers on the idea that racism is systemic in America. Racism in America is not only systemic, it is entrenched and persists to this day to help maintain the dominance of white people. It is an enduring feature of American life. Long overdue, the Critical Race Theory is not an "academic concept." It's history revisited and restored.

◆

We should be careful not to rhapsodize the "Founding Fathers." The liberty, equality, and justice they advocated were self-directed and narrow, not universal. They were all landowners dedicated to capitalist ideals, including the *"right to property"* which, by its very essence, excludes those who own nothing (the slaves) and those from whom (Native Nations) that property (America) was stolen. Forty-one of the fifty-six signers of the Declaration of Independence owned slaves. One of Jefferson's policies was to push *"Indians"* to the other side of the Mississippi River and to kill those who resisted. His Constitution is a telling document that should be understood by what it does not say. When the "Founding Fathers" wrote ... *"to establish Justice, ensure domestic Tranquility, provide for the common defense, promote the general Welfare, and secure the Blessings of Liberty to ourselves and our Posterity,"* they meant for *"us"* — White Anglo-Saxon Protestants proprietors — not *them*, for the white privileged classes, not the low-born landless masses, the slaves, or the aboriginal tribes they dispossessed, displaced, and massacred.

To those who claim that America "has changed," I argue that after a long and muted but troubled slumber, America bared its fangs and revealed itself for what it always was: racist, xenophobic, jingoistic, greedy, and boorish, at once phonily puritanical and insatiably promiscuous, hopelessly parochial, and loudmouthed. The fictitious image that the U.S. has of itself (and which it trumpets around the world) is a propagandist lie that many are determined to enshrine — damned be the truth.

Former President Jimmy Carter recently noted that throughout its history, America had enjoyed only sixteen years of peace, making it, as he wrote, *"the most warlike nation in the history of the world."* Since 2001, the U.S. has spent over $6 trillion on military operations and war, money that should have been invested in domestic priorities. It took the election and reelection of the first Black president to lift the mask and expose America's ugly face for all to see. On the eve of the one-year anniversary of the January 6, 2021, assault on the U.S. Capitol, Carter warned in a New York Times article:

> *"I now fear that what we have fought so hard to achieve globally — the right to free, fair elections, unhindered by strongman politicians who seek nothing more than to grow their own power — has become dangerously fragile at home."*

◆

Donald J. Trump is the incarnation of an unholy gestation and even after his ouster is now the source of all our fears and uncertainties. He breathes to trigger and cultivate antipathies, demonize his challengers, justify the hatred he exhales with every word he utters. His main tool of governance is the lie. Repulsive as he may be, Trump is less the cause of America's decline than a consequence of its downward spiral. To live under him while in full possession of one's faculties is to be in a perpetual state of rage and despair.

Of course, if you're white, healthy, steadily employed, have money in the bank, perhaps a few shares of some blue-chip stock in your portfolio, America is the Land of Cockaigne. It will not stay that way for long. Any suggestion that faith (the illogical belief in the occurrence of the impossible) and hope (an antidote for reality) alone can help reverse the catastrophic situation in which planet Earth finds itself is, at best, naïve, at worst, disingenuous and misleading.

A nation's economy can be said to be healthy only when all its citizens can enjoy its fruits, not just its privileged classes. The existence and proliferation of a small clique of multibillionaires who profit from the toil of the masses refutes the very notion of a healthy economy.

◆

If readers know anything about cults, they'll understand why, against all logic and despite the glaring evidence of strong-armed exploitation and abuse by their leaders, cult members have a hard time letting go. Trump provided his followers, indoctrinated in a cult of emperor worship, with an ideological coat of mail knitted to protect them against the heresy of truth and logic: Do not think. Do not question. Do not defy. Or else. Preprogrammed as they were by the lies they had absorbed since childhood, by the anti-Semitism spread by the New Testament (John in particular), and by generations of supremacist trash, it was easy for them to be seduced by a dangerous nobody like Trump.

◆

Is it any wonder that Christofascists invoke the Gospel of John, the most venomous anti-Semitic biblical tract that uses the word "Jews" sixty-three times — thirty-one times with rank hostility? The enemies of Jesus are described collectively as "the Jews," in contradistinction to the other evangelists who do not generally blame "the Jews" for the death of Jesus ... but don't express much fondness for them either. In the other three texts, the plot to put Jesus to death is always presented as coming from a small group of priests and rulers, the Sadducees. The Gospel of John continues to provide anti-Semites with grist for their mill. It is the primary source for the image of "the Jews" acting collectively as the enemy of Jesus, which later became fixed in Christian minds. It's all claptrap but for those who believe ... it's manna from heaven, it's comfort food. Apparently, inventing "God" was not enough. So, people invented his "son," born of *"immaculate conception"* (which is why Joseph, who may or may not have impregnated Mary and was replaced by the *"holy spirit,"* soon disappears from biblical texts.

◆

Democracy is imperfect and ultimately self-destructive because it tolerates in its very bosom the existence and proliferation of undemocratic ideas, people, and institutions. Short of a "benevolent" dictatorship that manages to reboot society (the stuff of vulgar utopias) we must find ways to make democracy work in our time. Alas, that will not prevent the future from spawning another Attila, Genghis Khan, Torquemada, Ivan the Terrible, Hitler, Mussolini, Stalin, Mao, Ceausescu, Pol Pot, Idi Amin, Victor Orbán, Jair Bolsonaro, Kim Jung Un, not to mention yet another Trump. Mankind is preprogrammed for eventual self-immolation and ensuing extinction. It's in our genes. Call it entropy.

The fanatical support (adulation is a better word) that Trump continues to enjoy among members of some 800 hate groups scattered across the U.S. can only be explained as a cultic fixation not unlike that of the followers of the Branch Davidians, the Manson family, the People's Temple (Jonestown, Guyana), and other equally self-deluded cliques. Donald Trump may be out of office, but his sect of violent white supremacists lives on and will quite possibly coalesce into a terrorist insurgency that will play a pivotal role in *"Making America Great Again."* They will all become more dangerous. Although they're likely to lose some numbers, they are frenzied hardliners and dead-enders, true believers, and they are probably going to be the source of a long-standing political and possibly paramilitary terrorist revolt. If nothing else, consider what a U.S. Army veteran said after she was arrested for taking part in the January 6, 2021 raid on the Capitol:

"I did what my president asked me to do." If that's not the kind of blind, unconditional submission displayed by cult followers, I don't know what is.

Past is prologue. It serves as a backdrop to the self-scripted science-fiction nightmare that has now entrapped us all. Keeping silent emboldens liars. A nation that trivializes or falsifies history does so at its own peril.

*"Colonialism: the enforced spread of the rule of reason.
but who is going to spread it among the colonizers?"*
— **Anthony Burgess (1917-1993)**

THE DEVIL'S DEPUTY—Social unrest (I was an early prognosticator of impending chaos) is simmering. Things will get a lot uglier. The U.S. is a nation adrift, rudderless, propelled by a tidal wave of hatred and now barreling towards the shoals of a national catastrophe. The assault on the Capitol was just a prelude. The Trumpeters were determined to invalidate the elections. House Speaker Nancy Pelosi, President-elect Joe Biden, and several Democratic and Republican members of Congress who had by now concluded that Trump was unhinged, were the targets of death threats. So was Trump's own vice president, Mike Pence. They all feared that Trump, in an act of suicidal revenge, might foment a national uprising or order an unprovoked nuclear attack against Iran or China in the final days of his presidency.

As these histrionics unfolded, and as Republicans, eager to ingratiate themselves with Jewish voters, rhapsodized their support for Israel, I got into a lengthy and acidulous tiff with "B," a former lieutenant of the late Rabbi Meir Kahane, the deranged activist who resorted to terrorism to combat anti-Semitism and who advocated the expulsion of Palestinians from Israel and occupied territories. Today a retired septuagenarian, "B" took umbrage at an editorial I had published in a Connecticut daily that excoriated then Prime Minister Benjamin Netanyahu and in which I expressed empathy for the Palestinian people. I had also quoted what a hawkish mid-level bureaucrat at Israel's Consulate General in New York, where I worked for a year as a press officer, said at a staff briefing on the prospects of peace:

> *"It is not in Israel's strategic interest to make peace with the Palestinians. To ensure Israel's total hegemony, we have no choice but to weaken the determination of the Palestinians through erosion, provocation, psychological warfare, expropriation, and colonization of occupied plots of land and, ultimately, the absorption of Palestinians into a Jewish State."*

I did not know at the time whether he was quoting official policy or engaging in wishful thinking. Angered, disappointed, I resigned my post within days. Diplomacy (politics/propaganda/deceit) and traditional journalism, I was now glaringly aware, are perilously incompatible, if not mutually exclusive. Condemned by the international community, Israel's posture, and subsequent events, seemed to validate the bureaucrat's astonishing avowals. I later learned that he was echoing the same Zionist mantra recited by Theodore Herzl, the father of Zionism; Zev Jabotinsky, founder of a new revisionist party whose stated objective was the establishment of a Jewish nation on both banks of the Jordan River; David Ben Gurion, Israel's first prime minister; Golda Meir, who served as the fourth prime minister of Israel from 1969 to 1974 and the first woman to become head of government in Israel; and Menachem Begin, founder of the ultra-right-wing Likud Party and the country's sixth Prime Minister.

Nothing has changed in the 74 years since Israel was founded. Its governing right wing fiercely opposes a two-state solution. Current Justice Minister, Gideon Sa'ar, a former deputy prime minister and a possible presidential contender, said recently:

> *"There is no two-state solution; there is at most a two-state slogan. It would be a mistake to return to the idea of establishing a Palestinian state in Judea and Samaria as a solution to the conflict."*

"B," whose reductionist philosophy is, *"If it's good for the Jews, that's all that matters...,"* hates Palestinians (she has never interacted with one) and loves Trump, who she never met but voted for. She was furious: She called me a self-hating Jew and lobbed the all-purpose slur — "communist." I rarely react to readers' kudos or brickbats, but "B's" manic affronts left me no choice. I let her have it with both barrels:

> *"If we don't see eye-to-eye it's because my life experiences — I am a Holocaust survivor, a student of History, a former servant in Israel's diplomatic corps, and a journalist — have predisposed me to viewing reality through a much wider, much clearer prism than yours."*

I am an avowed Jew, conscious and alarmed by the rise of fascism in the U.S. A "Kristallnacht," long thought impossible in pre-war Germany, I now fear, could precede the outbreak of anti-Semitic riots right here in America the Beautiful.

There are more than 800 registered hate groups in the U.S. — skinheads, neo-Nazis, xenophobes, anti-immigration, anti-gay, and violent misogynists. All were heavily represented at the storming of the Capitol, all responding to Trump's repeated calls to march on Washington and wrest the country back from the clutches of the *"Democrat Socialist Commies who want to take our guns, our states' rights, and our confederate flags."* I challenged her to mention one thing that Trump has done for the Jews — other than sow fear in their hearts that the Proud Boys, Aryan Nation, KKK, American Vanguard, Bomb Islam, American Nazi Party, Committee for Open Debate about the Holocaust, Soldiers of Odin (just to mention a few) might try to finish Hitler's job. Fixated on her ethnic identity, "B," it was obvious, had bought into and found herself trapped in a web of lies.

"B" changed course, arguing that Trump's unilateral and capricious recognition of Jerusalem as the undisputed capital of Israel was "good for the Jews."

I disagree. Jerusalem is no more the capital of Israel than it is the exclusive domain of Christendom or Islam. Instead, it has become the epicenter and bloodstained symbol of the discord and hatreds that only politics, dogmatism, and religious fanaticism can spawn. Yes, Netanyahu and his extreme right-wing cronies were elated: Trump had given them a political victory while making himself the darling of the ultra-Orthodox firebrands and settler movement. Many in Israel, including my own relatives, are appalled and fearful that this political charade will further aggravate tensions between Israelis and Palestinians. It did. Meanwhile, as the Palestinians, outnumbered, marginalized, strangers in their own land, are struggling to preserve fragments of their shrinking patrimony, new synagogues are rising on confiscated land. I could go on.

It is often not what we see but what we don't see (or refuse to look at) that colors our optic. Deeply ingrained, inflexible opinions tend to distort reality. They blind us and, carried to the extreme, render us mad. The unwillingness to put oneself in other people's shoes also does the truth great harm. While I emphatically support "Never Again," I reject the means used to enforce this chant. We should be well passed the savage Biblical *"An eye for an eye, a tooth of a tooth"* mindset. What terrified me about "B's" views, which include rabid homophobia, is that they are suffused with hatred and premised on payback.

A Cartesian dialogue with "B" was unlikely. She buries the truth under tons of falsehoods and propaganda concocted by the religious right to justify Israel's expansionist policies. It takes honesty and moral courage to judge history not as one imagines it (or as one wishes it to be) but as it is. I made three tactical errors: "B's" peripheral vision is corrupted by fanaticism; she never heard of Descartes; trying to reason with a zealot is a fool's errand. I am a journalist. My mission is to find the truth, wherever it may hide and despite the rancor my forays engender. Death threats have failed to deter me. The massacre of nine-tenths of my family in Hitler's slaughterhouses has taught me what extremism, in any form, can lead to. I also learned that dastardly acts can be justified by claiming self-defense ... or divine decree. The Jews became a threat to Germany's *"Aryan"* civilization. Palestinians became a threat to the colonization, by force, of the lands on which they lived for centuries. I refer to the violent expulsion of more than 400,000 Palestinians shortly after Israel's founding in 1948, and the assassination of more than 1,000 Palestinians in the past decade—many *"preemptive."* Assassination remains an official tool in Israel's arsenal of retributive policies.

I would understand the scope of these colonizing strategies only after poring over the correspondence between Theodor Herzl and British Prime Minister Arthur Balfour (1848-1930), author of the Balfour Declaration supporting the establishment of a *"national home for the Jewish people in Palestine,"* as well as the secret dispatches between Ben-Gurion, Begin, and Golda Meir who all declared, *"There is no Palestine,"* and the U.S. These dispatches are unambiguous.

Have we Jews, after millennia of persecution, exodus, dispersal, and near-extermination, forgotten what it is like to be second-class citizens? Or are we replaying the very horrors that led to the erection of a new nation on the usurped foundation of an existing homeland? Had we agreed to go to Uganda instead, would we have subjugated its native tribes, stolen their land, destroyed their homes and inflicted ruthless military rule?[7] Is the urge to avenge our ghastly past so irresistible that we are willing to commit the same crimes that earned us, for a time, the sympathy of the world? The suggestion that criticism of Israel is elementally anti-Semitic is a canard peddled by people whose selective memory has deprived them of a conscience. Such insinuation is sickening.

As for the *"Abraham Accords,"* as the U.S.-facilitated peace treaty normalizing relations between the United Arab Emirates and Israel is called, they came after months of debate over Israel's stated threat to annex parts of the West Bank, a move that would prevent a two-state solution to the Israeli-Palestinian conflict from ever being reached.

The absurdist claim that the Accords "improve the lives of the Palestinian and Israeli people," also pinpoint areas of the West Bank to be ceded to Israel, thereby encouraging Israel to unilaterally annex these territories without offering concessions in exchange. Smoke and mirrors.

For years, a persistent argument in the Palestine-Israel discourse has held that while Israel is not a perfect democracy, it is nonetheless a *"democracy for the Jews."* While the pillars of a true democracy include equality and justice, the latter maxim has given some plausibility to the argument that Israel can still strike a balance between being nominally democratic while remaining exclusively Jewish. This fragile argument is problematic. Even in the eyes of many Israeli Jews, the Israeli government no longer possesses democratic ideals. Indeed, Israel is a regime of Jewish supremacy "from the Jordan River to the Mediterranean Sea."

---

[7] The "Uganda Scheme" was a proposal presented at the Sixth World Zionist Congress in Basel in 1903 by Zionism founder Theodor Herzl to create a Jewish homeland in a portion of British East Africa. He presented it as a temporary refuge for Jews to escape rising antisemitism in Europe.

"B" openly professes that *"people who do not contribute to society"* have no rights — temporal and existential. Betraying a ghoulish form of chauvinism, she views Palestinians (as does Israel's right-wing Likud Party) as a *"sinister and divisive element."* This optic continues to invigorate the religious Right, whose enormous financial resources underwrote Benjamin Netanyahu's campaigns and whose gluttonous territorial expansionist objectives he and his cronies obsequiously bowed to.

It was the contrived 1948 "creation" of the State of Israel (as was the British engineered partition of India a year earlier, that split the country into two independent and forever warring dominions: India and Pakistan, the latter further separated from Bangladesh by a distance of 2,000 miles)[8] that changed the equation. Should we rid the world of certain aboriginal populations because they did not invent the wheel, spawn a da Vinci, a Beethoven, or an Einstein, or because what Palestinians aspired to before the "Nakba" was to cultivate their dunams, tend their orchards, raise their goats, and press their olives?[9]

◆

None is as blind as those who refuse to see. Like all confused individuals, "B," a self-described atheist, endorses the theocratic stranglehold that rabbis have on life in Israel. I urged her one last time to come out of her ideological cavern, to look deep into herself, and face facts: Trump is a crook, a pathological liar, a dangerous megalomaniac, a rabid xenophobe who fragmented

---

[8] Iraq and Jordan were also created after World War I from former Ottoman dominions by way of a secret bilateral agreement between the United Kingdom and Ireland, and the French Third Republic. Syria is considered to have emerged as an independent country for the first time in 1945.

[9] Nakba (Arabic) "disaster," "catastrophe," or "cataclysm," a word that reflects how Palestinians view the destruction of their homeland in 1948, when Israel was founded.

the U.S., an anti-Semite—his slumlord father long before him—backed, no, adored, by fascists and neo-Nazis, all armed to the teeth, and whose members (under orders from Trump), stormed the Capitol and planned to assassinate the vice president , the Speaker of the House, and Democratic members of Congress.

"If you believe that Trump really loves the Jews, I will sell you the Eiffel Tower. As for Israel, whose existence I support unreservedly, all I've ever asked of it is to show compassion," I concluded. I never heard from "B" again. One of the symptoms of ignorance and stupidity is an overabundance of preconceived ideas.

Rule No. 1: Resist the urge to reason against ignorance or stupidity. Some people are allergic to the truth. They would rather cling to fairy tales. Rule No. 2: Resist the temptation to believe that otherwise so-called *"decent folks"* are honest, altruistic, or kind. They can turn on you like a pit-bull on a poodle in the blink of an eye.

"Civil disobedience is not our problem.
Our problem is civil obedience …
while the jails are full of petty thieves…
and the grand thieves are running the country."
— **Howard Zinn (1922-2010)**

THE HIGH PRICE OF LOWERED EXPECTATIONS — Who will object to my characterization of Donald Trump as a dictator but the very people who eagerly swallow his lies and salivate like Pavlov's dogs whenever he opens his mouth? If I liken Trump to Hitler, it's because I've seen it all before — the enraptured mobs, the banners and unfurled flags, the martial posture, the body language, the anger that suffuses his rants, and the veiled threats they telegraph. His gatherings have all the trappings (and sounds) of a Nazi Party rally. Like Hitler, he is a shrewd and sinister shyster. America has everything to fear if he is reelected. Yet his fans, the blind leading the blind, swept in an irresistible momentum reminiscent of a wildebeest stampede, rush toward the precipice.

Empires rise, decline, and ultimately fall. Entropy is at work even in the best of times. There is no logical reason to assume that America won't go by way of the Sumerians, Phoenicians, Incas, Mayas, and Aztecs. Classical Greece, the cradle of democracy, disintegrated. So did Rome. So will this 246-year-old *"experiment."*

Tragically, about 43 percent of America's electorate will cheerfully vote to reelect Trump … which, should he win, will result in the persecution, incarceration (or "disappearance") of those who didn't vote for him. And he will play the fiddle while the nation burns. I don't have to tarry on the unravelling of America and the sense of foreboding about the future. Trump was openly, shamelessly admitting that he would resort to dirty tricks, if necessary, to insure a victory in November 2020. He had even signaled that people in red states should vote twice — which of course is illegal—and that armed "citizen militias" (translation: racist, neo-Nazi, anti-Semitic Christian crusaders) would ensure his victory. Being a "patriot" in today's America means you can shoot peaceful demonstrators and beat up people who advocate wearing masks, encourage vaccination, and support social distancing as the pandemic drags on. You can also assault Asians because they are singly and collectively responsible for the spread of the Covid-19. Democrats are now being labeled *"socialist terrorists."* The pro-Trump propaganda has reached a fever pitch. This is not mere idiocy. It's criminal insanity.

◆

I had never seen such a level of verbal and physical savagery. The coronavirus was in large part responsible for the angst and anger that are sweeping the nation, but I also recognized the resurfacing of an unmistakable trait: racism and a taste for violence. Six million Americans are unemployed. About four million are homeless. An equal number are behind prison walls, the majority people of color. The cost of living keeps rising. Food prices are soaring. Covid-19 continues to sicken hundreds of people every day. Nobody fully understands its etiology; no one knows how long it will last; and an incompetent leadership, more interested in kick-starting a dying economy than saving lives, is adding to the chaos. We'll be going to hell if America's Caligula is reelected. Where are Marcus Brutus and Cassius Longinus, I mused now that we really need them? The ballot box has since made tyrannicide superfluous. That is, if people vote their conscience instead of their prejudices.

◆

The glow past the black hole in which we're stuck will surge and spread when enlightenment and wisdom prevail. Right now, we're at the singularity's darkest point. If past is prologue, the climax is preordained and inevitable. The Second Law of Thermodynamics—more specifically entropy—states that organisms (we are after all "organisms") evolve from abundance to scarcity, from order to chaos, from equilibrium and symmetry to imbalance, from being to nothingness. Add to the mixture the global spread of fascism, rising poverty, growing pockets of famine, economic inequality, injustice, global pollution, wars, and pandemics … and what we have is a recipe for a bouillabaisse of troubles. Images from childhood stored in my mind's eye and those accumulated over the years only reinforce my view that we are all royally screwed. Blessed are those who still believe in the tooth fairy, Santa Claus, and the American Dream.

Problem is that, adding to Trump's absurd claim that America must be made "great" again to return to some semblance of normalcy (when were things ever normal?) so that billionaires can become trillionaires and the masses can indulge in their favorite pastimes—public drinking, sports events, rock concerts, beach parties, family reunions—the common folk are rebelling. Crowds of true-blue patriots demanding their second-amendment rights are demonstrating everywhere. Social distancing measures, they bellow, are unconstitutional as they infringe on their God-given right to get sick and infect others which, like the right to bear arms, is sacrosanct in this disunited United States. Sixty-six years in the U.S. and I still think I've crash-landed on a very strange planet

> *"People talk about the "bestiality" of man.*
> *no animal could ever be so cruel*
> *as a man, so artfully, so artistically cruel."*
> **—Fyodor Dostoyevsky (1821-1881)**

VOYAGE OF THE DAMNED—Time flies and memories are temporarily submerged under the weight of life's travails. But they return to haunt us.

Last December marked the anniversary of a now-forgotten event, the first of two incomprehensible acts of mass murder. Both would be eclipsed by the convulsions of a world at war, then trivialized by the passage of time. In retrospect, they would remind us of Russia's characteristic indifference to human life.

On December 12, 1941, fleeing the pogroms in Nazi-occupied Romania, 778 Romanian and Russian Jews embarked in the Black Sea port of Constanza on a small vessel of dubious seaworthiness, the SS Struma, bound for then British-controlled Palestine.

All too eager to rid his country of the Jews, the crossing had been approved by Romania's fascist dictator and convicted war criminal, Ion Antonescu. Passengers had each paid $1,000 (about $20,000 in today's currency) to make the voyage.

When they boarded, they were shocked to discover a greasy, dilapidated rust bucket. Sleeping quarters were primitive, filthy, and camped. There were only two lifeboats. Worse, the engine did not work. It had been salvaged from a wreck dredged from the bottom of the Danube River and hastily installed in the Struma's bowels.

Adrift for three days, the ship was towed to Istanbul, where it remained at anchor while "secret negotiations" between Hitler and his Turkish puppet were being held over the fate of its human cargo. With diminishing food and water reserves, lacking basic sanitation, conditions on the Struma worsened.

On the evening of February 23, 1942, after 70 days at sea, the disabled ship was seized by the Turkish police and towed through the Bosporus into open waters where it continued to drift.

At dawn a single torpedo launched from a Russian submarine tore into the Struma, splitting it in half. The jubilant submarine crew sent a self-congratulatory cable boasting that the "enemy vessel was successfully sunk from a distance of 1,118 meters and sunk." That day 103 children, 269 women, and 406 men died, among them two members of my family.

Before dawn on August 5, 1944, sailing under the Turkish and Red Cross flags, the Mafkura, a motor schooner chartered to carry Romanian refugees to Istanbul, was suddenly illuminated by flares from an unidentified vessel.

The Mefkura failed to respond and sailed on. It was soon fired on and sunk. Only five of the 350 passengers survived. Like the Struma, the Mefkura, it was later learned, had been torpedoed by a Russian submarine.

In-you-face prime-time images of man's inhumanity to man don't lie. Our world, history and the evening news remind us, is a sewer in which we wade knee-deep in the blood of martyrs. Gathered around the dinner table, we watch them die or fade away like ghosts. We owe it to our fragile, overtaxed psyches to forget an endless stream of atrocities — the Crusades, the "Holy" Inquisition, the wholesale massacre of native Americans, the Armenian genocide, the Holocaust, Biafra, the intertribal Hutu-Tutsi carnage, the U.S.-sponsored bloodbaths in Chiapas and the Guatemalan highlands, Bosnia, the 74-year-old Israeli-Palestinian bloodletting, Sudan, Iraq, Afghanistan, and the ongoing assassination of Central American street children by agents of the state.

These horror shock us to our core and remind us of our own mortality. The images we replay in our minds are reinforced by a steady diet of gruesome reminders compliments of our TV networks. Then fatigue sets in — emotional exhaustion. We tire of the spectacles that had kept us briefly spellbound and anguished. Distance, racial differences, and cultural incongruities all help intellectualize other peoples' agony. We endure it by purging our souls after each infamy.

"You can't change human nature," we pontificate, as we partake of dessert. In a pinch, a mind-numbing sitcom will help set our minds at ease. We survive the truth by looking the other way.

"When crimes begin to pile up, they become invisible.
When sufferings become unendurable, the cries are no longer heard.
The cries, too, fall like rain in summer."
— Bertolt Brecht (1898-1956)

GENOCIDE BY ANY OTHER NAME — I was eight in 1945 when my father, who had just learned that his parents and two brothers had perished in Auschwitz, sat me on his lap and gave me an unforgettable history lesson. "It's not the first time; it won't be the last," he whispered as he stroked the back of my head. "We forget the past until it reappears when we least expect it." He then spoke about an event — he called it a massacre — that had taken place when he was ten and which would be coined "genocide" in 1944.

Genocide is "the premeditated expulsion and mass murder of a people because of its indelible identity — race, ethnicity, religion, culture, and language." I choose this definition over others for its clarity and latitude.

The Armenian Genocide, also known as the Great Calamity, refers to the forcible deportation and slaughter of about 1.5 million Armenians during the Young Turks regime (1915-17) in the Turkish-ruled Ottoman Empire. Turkey steadfastly rejects the characterization of the events as "genocide" on semantic grounds and to serve self-justifying political, religious, and revisionist agendas.

The event is widely acknowledged as one of the first modern mass exterminations, and many sources point to the sheer scale of the death toll as evidence of a methodical scheme to thin out or eliminate an entire people.

Known to have inspired Hitler, it is the second most studied case of genocide after the Holocaust. Responding to Turkish denials, twenty-two nations and forty U.S. states adopted formal resolutions acknowledging the Armenian genocide as a bona fide historical event. Alabama, Indiana, Mississippi, Iowa, Wyoming, South Dakota, and West Virginia did not.

In 1896, The New York Times quoted a Turkish embassy gazette which, in a crass attempt at deflecting blame, alleged:

"It wasn't the Ottoman Court that caused the massacres in Armenia, but Christian propaganda in Asia Minor where the cry, 'Down with Islam' triggered the war of the crescent against the cross."

After a series of mass executions, The Times noted an apparent "policy of extermination directed against Christians in Asia Minor."

In 1909, as the authority of the nascent Young Turk government splintered, 30,000 Armenians perished during the Adana Massacre. By November 1914, the Ottoman Empire, which began to portray Armenians as a threat to Turkey's security, entered WWI on the side of Germany, Austro-Hungary, and Bulgaria. In 1915, Turkey rounded up, imprisoned, and later executed 250 Armenian intellectuals. That year, the cabinet passed an Inquisition-style Law of Expropriation, legalizing the deportation of Armenians and ruling that all property, including land, livestock, and homes belonging to Armenians, were to be seized.

By August 1915, The New York Times reported that "the roads and the Euphrates are strewn with corpses of exiles, and those who survive are doomed to certain death. Theodore Roosevelt characterized the carnage as "the greatest crime of the war." Describing it as a holocaust, Winston Churchill wrote:

"There is no reason to doubt that this crime was planned and executed for political reasons. The opportunity presented itself for clearing Turkish soil of a Christian race opposed to all Turkish ambitions."

Despite overwhelming evidence, denial by successive Turkish regimes continue to this day. Out of political expediency, other governments, including—inexplicably—Israel, aided and abetted Turkey in rewriting history.

Fast forward. In 2007, then Secretary of State Condoleezza Rice and Defense Secretary Robert Gates, signed an open letter to Congress, warning that formal recognition of the Armenian Genocide "could harm American troops in the field" by "antagonizing Turkey."

On October 20, 2007, prior to a vote by the House that officially condemned the events as genocide, Rice insisted the measure be defeated to "protect American regional interests and maintain basing rights in Turkey for American efforts in Iraq." By rejecting the resolution, the Bush administration demonstrated that it was less interested in morality than in its strategic self-interests. The claim by Senate Minority Leader Mitch McConnell that an *"event 100 years old does not merit revisiting"* is absurd and contemptible.

◆

I have always assumed that men prefer to be ruled by monsters than angels. How to explain the huge numbers of fanatic disciples that men like Attila, Genghis Khan, Hitler, Stalin, Mao, Saddam, the Kim—even Trump—were able to rally and transfix. I have also often proposed that the masses favor fairy tales over the naked truth, religion over science, apathy over action. And if the number of smart and virtuous people were in the millions instead of an amorphous minority, their influence on the rest of humankind would be just as insignificant. The Second Law of Thermodynamics suggests not only the progression from a state of abundance to one of scarcity, but, with it, a gradual state of decay that ultimately leads to chaos and collapse. While some smart people tend to get smarter, idiots get dumber and more prone to embrace totalitarian ideals and elect wicked men.

From this very unscientific but nagging speculation, one might then infer that even in the best of circumstances, most humans are inclined to terminal imbecility, a contagious disorder that a shrinking number of sane men and virtuous geniuses will be unable to thwart. Having said that, I will stick to my conviction that worrying about things over which I have no control is counterproductive and dumb. There is nothing that the smart people of this world can say that will make one bit of a difference in my life. If the warnings of visionaries like Isaiah, Jeremiah, Habakkuk, Daniel, Ezekiel, etc., had no effect during their lifetime, today's real prophets, scientists, are powerless against the chronic deafness of today's political miscreants and their acolytes. There is great deal of poetry in the Bible, some verifiable history, insight into the mindset of people in antiquity, practical advice, and tons of nonsense designed to enslave people mentally and paralyze them intellectually. Predictably, the more enormities and theatrics, the more the "faithful" believe. Man is not swayed by fact. He prefers histrionics, arcane gestures, and fairy tales

*"When Henry IV came to Paris he came
as a king who had conquered the people.
Now we are a people who have conquered the king."*
—**A Paris newspaper, July 1789.**

OFF WITH THEIR HEADS—I take wicked pleasure in reminding people that, on July 14, 1789, a ragtag band of derelicts, hoboes, petty thieves, and beggars armed with pitchforks, pikes, hatchets, cleavers, and their bare knuckles stormed the Bastille and, in one fell swoop, caused the fall of an absolute monarchy, a corrupt, sycophantic nobility, a venal clergy, and a thieving merchant class, all of which had, for centuries, sucked the marrow of millions of starving Frenchmen. Circulated at the time, a political cartoon depicted a dapper nobleman and a smiling, overfed cleric riding on the back of an old, exhausted peasant. The metaphor, pithy and painfully germane, had special resonance in 18th century France. Eons of misery and pent-up antagonism against the ruling aristocracy lit the fire of populist fury and took that nation from serfdom to democracy, from obedience to the Pope to the indissoluble partition between church and state.

Yes, a few royal heads and skulls of lesser distinction rolled into the wicker baskets at the foot of the guillotine, but France was rid, for the first time in its history, of vampires and scoundrels, and was well on its way to the fiercely secular, socialist republic it is today. Much like the Russian Revolution, which had begun to simmer but would not erupt for another century, the French Revolution was a grassroots-inspired insurrection fueled by centuries of oppression, exploitation, and corruption at the hands of dynasties of all-powerful, greedy, war-mongering thugs. Seen in a modern context, the French satirical drawing says much about 21st century America. It rings a strident bell with the coalescing voices of discontent and reminds all of us that there can be no privileged elite without an abused underclass.

The prognostications I allowed myself to make in my play were coming true.[10] A dangerous sociopath had been occupying the White House. Should he be reelected, everyone agreed, he would spend his second term exacting vengeance on those who opposed him, contradicted him, mocked him. If he loses, he will refuse to accept the will of the people. Ethno-nationalism in times of partial democracy is a combustive mix that often triggers insurrection. There will be blood.

So, the question remains: Is "peaceful transition" an anachronism, a paradigm of political inertia and collective cowardice? How come Americans did not storm the White House, yank the rascal out of bed, and march him to some makeshift gallows? How come, after more than a year out of office, he still commands more than 40 percent of the electoral vote? Can one safely argue that he is no longer the problem but that the terminal imbecility of his followers (and the inertia of his detractors) is what we must fear should he choose to run again instead? Never has there been a more urgent need for a nation that has lost its moral compass, to lead a moral revolt. France, the country that shuts down or sets itself on fire when the leaders piss the people off, a man like Trump couldn't, wouldn't have been appointed dog catcher, let alone president. And if by some incomprehensible twist of fate, he had been elected, he wouldn't have lasted a month in office. He would have then been unceremoniously ousted or sent to Devil's Island.

The U.S. Capitol insurrection was far from a self-contained day of rage. It was both the culmination of the rule of an aberrant, demagogic President and a catalyst for the most enduring onslaught on America's system of elective governance

---

[10] *One Last Dream* (© 2012 – CCB Publishing).

in decades. It legitimized violence as a tool of political expression among millions of citizens and cast the haunting possibility that as horrific as that day was, it may be only a preview of a deeper democratic rupture to come.

> *"Schools serve the same social functions*
> *as prisons and mental institutions –*
> *to define, classify, control, and regulate people."*
> **— Michel Foucault (1926-1984)**

IF HATRED WAS A FUEL—Life in the shadow of the coronavirus seems to have lost all meaning. It's now a matter of enduring each day as it comes, with so far unrealistic hopes for a better tomorrow. Meanwhile, Trump is showing growing signs of psychosis. He lies with every word he utters. He attacks the media, threatens those who disagree with him, and is now issuing new directives that are retaliatory and that further weaken America's enfeebled democracy. And, yes, his popularity has not diminished and his chances of reelection, while slimmer than before, cannot be ruled out. What makes a vulgar, unhinged, mean-spirited crook so appealing to more than 40 percent of America's electorate is beyond comprehension. A possible explanation is that the 40 percent are 100 percent illiterate and mean-spirited yahoos. The remaining 60 percent are sitting on their thumbs and waiting for Godot. Never has a national leftist insurrection been more pressing than now. But those who have a job, a roof over their heads, and can still afford to eat feel no urgency to act; the others are busy surviving an unending battle against economic collapse and creeping destitution. Entropy in its most basic manifestation.

It's anyone's guess. But the toxic mixture of Covid-19, unemployment, inflation, racism, and signs of Trump-fatigue, that is growing dissatisfaction with his presidency, lies, and fascist leanings, could provide the spark for a major, nationwide uprising ... which would immediately be met with massive military retaliation ... and further shrinking of a comatose democracy. Cops and national guardsmen have never shied from shooting at civilians and I'm not sure that Americans have the courage or the firepower to do what a ragtag band of hoboes, derelicts, and petty thieves armed with pikes, rakes, knives, cleavers, and their bare fists did on July 14, 1789, when they stormed the Bastille.

Trump has become a dangerous and polarizing figure. I am more inclined to speculate that either a victory or a defeat at the polls in November will result in major unrest—with a defeat sparking greater bloodshed.

None of this, though, should come as a surprise. Here was America's police—killing hated minorities on the streets, repeatedly, in horrific ways. Caught on video. This one strangled, that one suffocated, the other shot in the back. Gun violence. Mass shootings in which nearly 19,000 men, women, and children were killed in 2022. The world is aghast. What has America become? The answer: America percolated into a pre-authoritarian nation for a decade or two, after making an abortive attempt at being a true democracy, which only lasted about 30 years. Before that, it was the world's largest apartheid state.

To the cries of "we want Trump, we want Trump" on January 6, 2021, American democracy stuttered and froze. Two months after the presidential election, the world was witnessing, incredulous and dumbfounded, the invasion of the Capitol by thousands of enraged demonstrators.

Adopting the tactics and language of the anti-abortion lobby, Trump, the pirate of democracy, reworked information he knew to be fake and belched it to the delight of his fans. For months he argued without evidence that the Democrats engineered a large-scale scheme to steal the 2020 election. Everyone knows by now that this ludicrous claim was not anchored in reality. All these denunciations of so-called fraud brought by Trump and his friends to the court of public opinion have since been put to rest.

But no matter, the damage was done. The poison of disinformation spreads on social media and is taken for Gospel truth (an oxymoron) by a disturbingly large number of Americans. Social networks could counter the spread of fake news, but it would cost them millions of dollars and the support of their audience and subscribers.

The enduring appeal and possible re-candidacy of Donald Trump begs the question: How far can we play with hate? His provocations and outlandish lies keep feeding a wellspring of extreme right-wing rhetoric. To the unprecedented media complacency, which allows this character to dominate the airwaves is added a plot that aims to accelerate the advent of a fascist state. Endorsing, legitimizing the likes of Donald Trump corrupts America's conscience and opens the door to the worst in man.

Explicit calls for the liquidation of left-wing figures is not mere rhetoric. Encouraged by the prime-time dissemination of its ideas far right agitators feel entitled to physically threaten those who do not think like them. Some said they were ready to act. Compared to America's Fox News, CNews, France's right-wing channel, buried the story but the arrest, in recent days, of identity activists who had a real arsenal proves that the U.S. is not immune to a Christchurch. Indeed. two years ago, Brenton Tarrant, who opened fire on Muslims in this New Zealand city, killing 51 people, admitted to being a follower of the *"great replacement,"* the bogus theory espoused by Trump and engraved in his hymnal.[11] In this writer's view, anyone guilty of inciting

---

[11] The white nationalist far-right conspiracy theory disseminated by French author Renaud Camus who states that, with the complicity or cooperation of left-wing elites, white European populations are being demographically and culturally replaced with non-white peoples—especially from Muslim-majority countries—through mass migration, demographic growth, and a drop in the birth rate of white Europeans.

hatred, right or left, is ineligible to hold public office. It is also his opinion that if hatred was a combustible capable of being poured into gas tanks, the world's energy crisis would be a thing of the past.

> *"The emphasis must be not on the right to abortion*
> *but on the right to privacy and reproductive control."*
> **—Ruth Bader Ginsburg (1933-2020)**

POTESTAS SEMPER VINCIT—Power always wins. A concerted battle against women's rights is now underway. By choosing to seize laws passed by red states restricting the use of abortion, instead of relying on the decisions of intermediate judicial bodies that had found it unconstitutional, the U.S. Supreme Court opened a breach against Roe v. Wade which enshrined this right in 1973. The purpose of faith-based laws prohibiting abortion before the threshold of viability is to challenge existing jurisprudence and abolish it by force.[12] There is nothing improvised about an offensive that crowns years of mobilization against the historic decision which protects the voluntary termination of pregnancy

Recent rulings by conservative states are symbolic assaults in a culture war that has been waged by America's religious right for nearly four decades. This war is being justified in the name of the sanctity of life that otherwise disappears dramatically from the conservative discourse when it comes to the death penalty, *"enhanced interrogation techniques"* (a euphemism for torture of detainees at remote sites around the world), and dirty wars. This obsessive mobilization has borne fruit by taking advantage of the inequities of America's electoral system. Donald Trump, elected president after losing the popular vote, appointed three judges chosen by the Federalist Society, a conservative lobby. The latter, appointed for life, were confirmed by Senate Republicans, mostly from rural and sparsely populated states. The conservative camp, now six anachronistic judges against only three progressives, has gained the upper hand. Although cautious as always in this matter, the interventions by judges

---

[12] *Potestas Semper Vincit:* Power always wins.

appointed by Republican presidents suggest that they could validate, regressive laws, thus paving the way for other challenges and, finally, for a questioning of the national scope of the right to abortion.

The price to pay for the Republican Party's ruthlessness against democracy will not be negligible. Such a reversal from the 1973 ruling, the latter having been reinforced by a second decision in 1992, would enshrine the politicization of one of the few institutions still relatively spared by the extreme polarization that currently makes the U.S. a model of blackjack political activism.

By legalizing same-sex marriage in 2015, another scarecrow of the conservative camp, the Supreme Court had intelligently accompanied a major evolution in American society. The latter has since been the subject of a solid consensus, including a significant part of the Republican camp. It would be quite different if the same Court were to pronounce itself in favor of a return to the right to abortion. The latter enjoys solid and stable public support, with 60 percent of favorable opinions (against 27 percent of contrary opinions). The conservative crusade against women's rights thus appears for what it is: the callous indifference by a group of ultra-conservative justices who, familiar with the arguments in support of abortion as a foundational right, shrug off the profound social, legal, and financial costs of forcing women to carry unwanted pregnancies to term. Whereas the Constitution does not provide for the right to abortion—it doesn't even mention the word—it does not ban it. These justices' decision is not anchored in law. It festers, unholy and noxious, the admixture of intolerance, dark nationalism, and the intoxicating rewards of personal power.

"The need to tell and hear stories is essential to the human species. The opposite of silence leads quickly to narrative, and the sound of story is the dominant sound of our lives, from the small accounts of our day's events to the vast uncommunicable constructs of psychopaths."
—Reynolds Price (1933-2011)

THE OPPOSITE OF SILENCE—What most of us can ever hope to know for certain is second-hand knowledge endlessly retold, recast, and misread: the idiosyncratic, hand-me-down, robotic indoctrinations to which we are subject from the youngest age; the expedient reinterpretations of history; the often slanted pedagogy of our teachers; the fanciful credos of religion; the partisan reflections of the press; and the falsehearted proclamations of our elected officials. What was once learned from instinct and direct personal experience has since been prepackaged into a one-size-fits-all view of the world suitably tinted to accommodate individual preconceptions, partialities, and traditions—not to debunk them. The clarity of truth is being mercilessly dimmed by the tendency to regard it as a doubt-free, black-or-white affair lacking grays, devoid of ambiguities, even of improbabilities that would stagger the mind if someone took the time to look, to think, to probe, to doubt.

We all need to hear stories. But, somehow, we're fond only of those that don't dispute our own accounts of reality, that don't threaten our ideological or emotional comfort zones. We've become so anesthetized by sanctioned reality that we overlook the colossal lies that "official" truths conceal. Worse, we don't bother to read between the lines. We refuse to extricate fact from cautionary tale. We allow hints of veracity to color our fantasies, to stimulate our adrenal glands—we're thrilled by the oblique suggestion of danger, horror, or salaciousness so long as these enticements remain abstract, so long as we're surrogates, vicarious onlookers, not partakers. Other people's stories help legitimize our voyeurism. The tales we spin betray our narcissism.

But what is a story? How is it conceived? Is it the product of mental parthenogenesis—inadvertent, spontaneous reproduce-tion—or is it an artifact, the handiwork of converging processes, such as intuition, the ability to form mental images of things that either are not physically present or have never been conceived, or revelation?

"Whoever yearns for freedom, justice and peace may rise again and raise his head, for in Christ liberation is drawing near." — Luke (21:28).

Somehow, that 2,000-year-old pledge turned out to be an empty, cruel ruse. The *"Savior"* saved nothing. Ours is the most violent, dysfunctional, and catastrophe-prone epoch in Earth's history. Hostilities are raging worldwide. Global warming and climate change are feeding droughts, fires, floods, crop failures, famine, and death. Animal loss of habitat, human overpopulation, and unfettered urbanization are emboldening the onset of plagues, among them Ebola and the coronavirus.

Isn't it time to stop reaching for the Moon (and Mars), pool the vast fortunes of a privileged few and address the pressing and persistent problems that now threaten the human race? Rhetorical question, of course. No one really gives a damn. Will people give up their gas-guzzling SUVs, their ocean-polluting cruises and air-poisoning intercontinental jet flights, their oil-coal- gas- and electric-based air conditioning and heating systems, their ravenous consumption of meat, their pesticides, their giga-malls, their large-screen TVs, and their suicidal procreative instincts? Not when money is at stake. Convulsing under rising waves of hatred, ignorance, superstition, and stupidity, plagued by mounting violence, the world still awaits salvation—from itself. Racked by poverty, despair, and ethnic strife, "emergent nations," those dirt-poor, underdeveloped countries we derisively called the "Third World," continue to be in desperate need of social justice, economic stability, and independence from their puppet-masters as they teeter on the brink of civil war or have already succumbed to it. In other parts of the world people struggle to preserve increasingly shrinking fragments if their ancestral homelands. Climate change puts arctic regions on thin ice, threatens to inundate coastal areas and engulf dozens of islands around the globe, while prairies wither and turn into dustbowls. Embroiled in unwinnable wars, at home and abroad, the U.S. clings to the two-party system, both parties indistinguishable one from the other except for the partisanships and antipathies they inspire, both tied to corporate wealth, both intent on blocking meaningful reforms, both beholden to Wall Street, both involved in larceny against the poor.

The gap between the haves and the have not continues to widen. The Catholic Church, the richest empire on earth and the self-anointed moral arbiter to millions, is embroiled is sordid scandals. Living in Babylonian splendor, donning richly festooned vestments, basking in the idolatrous reverence of the flock, "princes" of the Church breathe the rarefied air of their own saintly afterlife and sneer at mankind's earthly needs. Not to be outdone, intoxicated by the apocalyptic rants found in Revelation, Evangelical Christians pray for an all-consuming Armageddon.

The crucifixion of Yeshua of Nazareth is a fitting metaphor for man's inhumanity. Alas, its commemoration reminds us that salvation, like justice, human rights, compassion, ethics, and love, remains a distant vision, not a serious objective.

Never honest with itself, history unfolds while historians deform it. One man's truth is another man's propaganda. The allure of history rests not always on the events it chronicles but in the chronicler's subjective interpretations. Without such "embroidery," the annals of man would consist of little more than a brief, uninspiring compendium of facts and dates. Whereas social scientists tend to interpret history as an evolution from savagery to emotional maturity and intellectual refinement, reality is far less reassuring. In the aggregate, human society seesaws wildly between states of stagnancy, feverish creativity, uneasiness, turmoil, and madness. Although these oscillations can be blamed on the cretins, kleptocrats, and killers we elect (or surrender to) they are hastened, prolonged, and fossilized by the appalling lethargy of the masses. As Voltaire was fond of saying, "History is a lie commonly agreed to." Yes, victors write history to justify and exalt conquest, losers to mitigate defeat. Neither side will concede the other's account. The hostility such divergence of opinion ignites leads to more acrimony, more violence, and more needless deaths that future historians will find of little interest and reduce to minutia.

In a story, as in a revolution, the greatest challenge is how to end it. In addition to bringing their own knowledge of history, storytellers must own up to it: An ending is not supposed to be a surprise. To envision a plausible finale, we must also reflect on the paroxysm of lunacy and violence that now convulse our planet.

> *"A body of men holding themselves accountable to nobody*
> *ought not to be trusted by anybody.*
> **—Thomas Paine (1737-1809)**

LIBERTARIANISM: A HOAX—Libertarianism is a sloppily coined, and deceptively marketed ideology that hallows *"the right of free choice."* It comes in two flavors. One masks the stench of *"inherent rights"* which disregard individual obligations and responsibilities. The other spices up *"individual rights"* with a heady bouquet of causal assumptions about what freedom is and how to secure it. Those who call themselves Libertarians confuse these seasonings, sometimes deliberately, often out of ignorance or self-induced frustration over real or perceived existential threats. The 18th century antiroyalist writers who inspired France and a nascent United States, advocated against despotism, not legitimate governance. Deliberately or unwittingly, ostensible Libertarian entitlements work against the greater good of all. This is the philosophical side of the argument. Reality casts an uglier light.

Neo-conservatives, with their own brand of anarchic fetichism, find an attractive political refuge in Libertarianism. It crowns them with a fake aura of patriotism, integrity, and tolerance. In fact, they believe that individual freedom endows them with the clear conscience to do what genuine democracy rebukes, like sedition, secessionism, and the circumvention of legitimate government oversight. Instead, it favors the imposition of capitalist norms on the whole of society. As such, Libertarianism is little more than a seductive fallacy structurally incapable of evolving a model of how to use freedom equitably. Its root dogma, that *"all free choices are equal,"* is a theory it cannot support without admitting that there are other virtues besides freedom. If Marxism can be viewed as the delusion that one can run society purely on altruism and collectivism, Libertarianism is the myth that one can govern, as Ayn Rand preached, purely on self-interest, laissez-faire, and isolationism. Like Marxism, but devoid of its oratorical eloquence, Libertarianism aspires to reduce social life to economics while making its followers feel like a "Chosen People" freed from the moral rules that guide the majority.

Libertarians utter simplistic slogans—*"We love freedom, we abhor tyranny."* Even when they attempt to define their credo, it is neither accurate nor honest. They claim that their system would produce desirable results. Arguing from results is not enough to justify a political ethos. The attitude of American and British fascists was caricatured in a famous one-liner: *"Mussolini cleaned up the bordellos and made trains run on time."* Libertarians favor a drastic deregulation and full privatization of the economy. They demand that individuals accept the outcome of market forces. They legitimize economic inequality and injustice by refusing to define it as a coercive force. Not unlike Evangelical Christians, they exploit the political process to penetrate it and ram through faith-based agendas that conceal dangerous attitudes:

> *"Capitalism is noble." "Worker activism and unions are evil." "The poor are pampered good-for-nothing freeloaders who deserve their fate." "'Equal rights' is a code word for socialism."*

This philosophy, if one can call it that, is largely embodied in Ayn Rand's capitalist tirades and Jefferson Davis' absurdities. Both Davis and Rand are the darlings of the neocons and modern anti-abolitionists. Rand exalted selfishness; she called it a "virtue." Davis referred to slavery as *"that peculiar institution"* and *"a steppingstone for the Negro to become perfect."* Libertarianism is a mindset adopted by a broad spectrum of rigid—not freethinking—individuals who clamor for "states' rights" and who would cheerfully curtail or abolish the freedoms of their challengers. Industrialists whose companies dump toxic wastes in oceans, rivers, and lakes also consider themselves Libertarians, as do those who would flood the country with assault weapons because they favor a free-market economy … but would criminalize stem-cell research, pot-smoking, abortion, and same-sex marriage to defend their high moral convictions.

Last, Libertarianism is a word that arouses stirring emotions. In truth the concept has been corrupted by profiteers and political mutineers to conceal an agenda of unrestrained capitalism and religious orthodoxy. Its most ardent—and dangerous—advocates once traded white hoods for teabags. On all these counts, Libertarianism simply doesn't stack up. Once people can see through the fog of deceptive politics, expect them to toss it out as a failure and a moral mess apt to pollute and disfigure society.

> *"The end of the human race will be that*
> *it will eventually die of civilization."*
> **— Ralph Waldo Emerson (1803-1882)**

THE FINAL CURTAIN—Humans are paradoxical life forms. Earth could be the only place in the universe with organisms capable of evolving creative geniuses like Beethoven, Shakespeare, and Michelangelo, evil enough to poison the likes of Genghis Khan, Torquemada, Hitler, Stalin, Mao and other monsters with unfathomable cruelty, dumb enough to believe in (and wackily promote) the grotesque absurdities that religion(s) shove down our throats, and craven enough to endure or champion the colossal but tempting lies on which politicians' careers are anchored. It was French philosopher, Gustave Le Bon (1841-1931), an otherwise fierce critic of democracy and socialism, who conceded:

> *"Whoever can supply the masses with illusions is easily their master; whoever attempts to destroy their illusions is always their victim."*

Illusions are as old as the hills, as ancient as our fear of the unknown, as compelling as the primordial urge to attack and destroy what we don't understand.

◆

Absolutist ideas keep humans keyed up and trigger-happy. Barring some catastrophic cosmic event or an all-consuming thermonuclear apocalypse, the human race will limp along and endure. In the grand scheme of evolution, the human brain could devolve (if it hasn't already) into a rudimentary organ, like the appendix, which serves no purpose: Worms (like humans) have proven that it is indeed possible to eat, defecate, and replicate without a brain. That's the fictional worst-case but not improbable scenario. Closer to current reality, and with Ukraine as a backdrop, U.S. sanctions, military aid ($55 billion and counting), and inflammatory rhetoric can be expected to trigger global shockwaves. The supply chains are dangerously strained and could collapse, causing inflation to spike and precipitating irreversible food shortages leading to starvation.

Unresolved military conflicts in Afghanistan, Syria, Iraq, Yemen, Libya, and Sudan; territorial disputes (Israeli-Palestinian; Russo-Ukrainian; Kurdish-Turkish) continue to smolder. Sectarian crises, political instability, and transnational terrorism are on the rise. The failure of international institutions to settle the situation in Ukraine, according to former Russian president and Deputy chairman of the Russian Security Council, Dmitri Medvedev,

"...could spur a new world order and the creation of new international alliances based on pragmatic rather than ideological Anglo-Saxon criteria." Medvedev also predicted *"the collapse of the idea of an American-centric world."*

This was not a prediction but a blueprint, especially after President Joe Biden suggested that Mr. Putin be tried for war crimes. The gaffe is so serious that, according to the latest intelligence, the U.S. is now closer to war with Russia than at any time, including the Cold War.

Addressing a meeting of the International Institute for Strategic Studies in Singapore, on June 11, 2022, U.S. Defense Secretary Lloyd Austin's somber warning leaves no room for speculation:

"Russia's invasion of Ukraine is what happens when oppressors trample the rules that protect us all. It's what happens when big powers decide that their imperial appetites matter more than the rights of their peaceful neighbors. And it's a preview of a possible world of chaos and turmoil that none of us would want to live in."

A day later, Yale historian Timothy Snyder, an expert on authoritarianism, published a lengthy Twitter thread explaining how he believes Russian President Vladimir Putin plans to starve some countries by using food insecurity to his advantage. Snyder called this strategy *"the latest chapter of hunger politics."* Snyder said he believes Putin's *"hunger plan"* had three main objectives. First, to cut off Ukraine's exports in an attempt to destroy its statehood. Second, to create instability in Europe by producing refugees from areas that rely on Ukraine's food, like North Africa and the Middle East:

> *"If the Russian blockade continues, tens of millions of tons of food will rot in silos, and tens of millions of people in Africa and Asia will starve."*

Sic transit gloria mundi.

> *"Most ignorance is vincible ignorance.*
> *We don't know because we don't want to know."*
> **—Aldous Huxley (1894-1963)**

POSTSCRIPT—I spent nearly a lifetime doggedly keeping the emperor naked for all to see in his shameless nudity. My exertions produced short-lived, insignificant ripples, not the tsunami of revulsion my polemics were intended to unleash. For humanity to survive and thrive, I had insisted, the radical ideas of one generation must eventually become the commonsense ideas of the next. The deeper we probe within ourselves, the more certain we become of the unreality of temporal free will. The only freedom we have is the contemplation of untested ideas. I was called a whiner. Telling inconvenient truths is risky business. I'd been in the trenches as tracer bullets whizzed over my head. I'd been grazed once or twice. Had my reflexes failed me when I exposed racism, political corruption, police brutality, and military crimes, I might not be whining today.

Much still begs to be said, revealed, dissected. Well-meaning people have urged me to *"veer away from the kind of truths that infuriate readers,"* to treat them instead *"to the bland fiction that spares them the hazards of hypertension and the compulsion to strike back."* Are these well-meaning cowards the readers' friend or mine?

Words survive briefly in the two-dimensional realm of an investigative report or opinion piece, but they fail to generate change. Instead, they leave a wasteland of rhetoric that does nothing to alter human nature, chill passions, and curb hatred. Some horrors are simply too shocking or too banal for words.

The truth is not a marketable commodity. I abandoned all pretenses that my words would ever stimulate a rational dialogue, let alone trigger change. Resorting to disinformation, a gaggle of right-wing moralizers who hide behind the anonymity of their blogs always strikes back, rejecting facts or trivializing them with puerile, spiteful, often malicious bursts of ad hominem attacks.

Is truth-telling worth the wall of odium and discord it raises? I struggle with this question with every commentary I pen. If it takes whining to ventilate inconvenient truths, so be it. I will whine. It helps clear my throat … and my conscience.

♦

My third eye, wide-open since childhood when I first became aware of man's evilness, now resurrected a scenario first staged in *One Last Dream*. I had written,

"Men 17 to 69 are in uniform, training for the front or patrolling the streets. Everyone is armed. The haves wrangle with the have-nots. Looting, assaults, and other spasms of violence soared during the long hot summer and thousands died at the hands of paramilitary squads, mercenaries, and gangs, all eager to settle scores. Justice is blind to injustice. Anti-war activists are inciting greater resentment against their cause by flag-waving diehards too old to be conscripted but misguided enough to raise the decibels of jingoism and sanctimony to ear-blasting heights. Basic staples — bread, milk, eggs — are in short supply. Meat, oh, what a horror, when available at black market prices, is rarely fresh. But hunger subverts reason; everyone takes chances. And while hunger and exposure kill the poor, it is often food poisoning that claims those who can still afford to eat. Not unlike ants, people spent the fall hoarding and digging in deeper. A calamitous winter, at best, lies ahead."

It was during another lucid dream — or was it my third eye forcing me to focus on the persistence and inalterability of reality — that I was reminded of the pointlessness of cautionary tales. Nobody listens. Nobody gives a damn. Nobody.

As I surveyed the dreamscape from the unobstructed heights of reason, I was also reminded that planet Earth is a place where some have more than anyone could ever need to live with dignity, while others have nothing. It's a realm in which good and evil are hotly contested and narrowly interwoven, where right and wrong feed upon each other with such voracity that neither wins nor loses so that both may emerge unscathed from their unholy symbiosis. It's a locale where a corrupt, craven, avaricious gerontocracy calls upon the very young to risk mutilation and insanity or to die in their stead. It's a place where wars are waged to break the monotony of peace, where combatants are feted for their homicidal deeds with medals and ribbons and boisterous parades, whereas common felons rot in stinking jails or swing from the gallows or fry on the electric chair. It's the halfway house where, left to their own devices, flawed but redeemable beings mutate into a race of cutthroats. It's the purgatory where a species of erect bipedal primates was exiled a quarter of a million years ago so that they might expiate their brutish ways.

Instead, they went to war *"to wrest the Holy Land"* from the apostate Jews and Muslims. They burned Giordano Bruno, Girolamo Savonarola, and Jacques de Molay alive for contradicting the Church's grotesque beliefs and ruthless mandates. Convicted as a "heretic," a label still used today to brand skeptics and truth-tellers, Joan of Arc suffered the same fate, only to be later beatified and canonized a *"saint"* by the same thugs who ordered her execution. Galileo Galilei, who championed Copernican heliocentrism (the Earth revolves round the Sun, not the other way around) was forced by the Inquisition to recant and died under house arrest a broken man. In an important sense, which can never impugn his genius or diminish his scientific achievements, the trial of Galileo is fascinating for the insights it provides into the inner workings of the Inquisition, an efficient, ruthless tribunal from whose diabolical secret procedures no one escaped unscathed once its wrath was aroused.

Inquisitors also burned books. Works by Europe's intellectual elites, among them Erasmus, Machiavelli, Dante, Voltaire, Rousseau, Descartes, Pascal, Spinoza, and Bocaccio—later Balzac, Dumas, Flaubert, Hugo, Sartre, and Zola—were repugnant to the Church and banned. Censorship, redaction, and expurgation had a disastrous effect on the development of scientific thought, philosophy, and art, as it does now in parts of the world where freethinking, erudition and tolerance, the cardinal virtue of righteous men, are considered unpatriotic or treasonous. It wasn't until 1966 that the Congregation for the Doctrine of the Faith abolished the Index, a list of publications deemed heretical, satanic, or contrary to morality, conceding that while the list maintained its moral force by teaching Christians to beware of writings that could dilute or extinguish their faith, it was no longer able to enforce it. Remarking on the fragility of religious faith and the lengths to which the Church would go to enforce it, Aldous Huxley wrote:

> *"The Inquisition burns and tortures in order to perpetuate a creed, a ritual, and an ecclesiastico-politico-financial organization regarded as necessary to man's salvation."*

His words were prophetic in what they augured: the rise of fanaticism and intolerance, and the methods fanatical and intolerant people devise to maintain the supremacy and protect the bounties their extremism bestow.

Inspired by intolerance, religious fanaticism, and the Vatican's virulent anti-Masonic injunctions and penalties— excommunication—an anti-Masonic crusade has resurfaced in America on two fronts. Fire and brimstone preachers can be heard mocking Freemasonry on AM and shortwave radio stations, and in places of worship across the country. The enormities they spout are as daft as they are false. But there is always an audience that can be made to believe anything. More insidious is the subtle desecration of tolerance that took decades to bear fruit when, veering away from its European roots, American Freemasonry stopped spreading "Light" and promoting social justice. It has since closed in on itself and turned into a citadel of far-right religious and political extremism. Worse, as religious fundamentalists continue to slander and defame the ancient fraternal order, and whereas it takes three years to be fully vested in Europe, new generations of Freemasons are initiated in three months ("90-day wonders") and are groomed into vectors of religious and political conservatism.

◆

No sooner had I embarked on a dizzying descent down history's spiral staircase than I found myself standing on the first rung. If the dream I spun is dystopic in its contemplation of the future, it is also a rear-view mirror in which the past unfolds in reverse all the way to the beginning of time.

At dawn, bipedal proto-human primates used their teeth, their claws. Later, they picked up a rock, a bough, an errant bone. They felt a power surge through their fists, and the carnage began. At high noon, bombs started to rain. Fragmentation bombs rip, slash. Incendiary bombs scorch. Concussion bombs produce shockwaves that shatter granite. Napalm, a combustible jelly, like molten lead, sticks to flesh and devours it.[13] Does anyone remember the grainy, black-and-white war footage of Kim Phuk, the Vietnamese little girl burned by napalm as she runs toward the cameraman crying in horror and agony?

---

[13] Manufactured by Dow Chemical, proud makers of mustard gas, agent orange, and dioxin.

Some bombs spread the plague. Others paralyze, suffocate, blind. Neutron bombs snuff out life but spare buildings, monuments, and shrines, Future munitions may target the poor, the sick, the mad. Some could be programmed to obliterate certain races. Skunk works might even be developing a precision device that wipes out all greying men who indulge in radical banter; ordnance that aims at those who can't help but feel that more bombs are on the way, who say so out loud, and who warn that there will soon be no good place left to hide.

♦

It began with a salvo of statements and counterstatements tailored to help adversaries save face at home while giving the rest of the world the impression that a global conflagration was inevitable and imminent unless the other side relented, War is often the result of miscalculation rather than plan, a strategy that often leads to unintended consequences. Neither side really waned war, you see, and no one was quite prepared to wage it, but in time., words got sharper, less conciliatory, and weapons — the antithesis of reason — grew deadlier with each statement and counterstatement.

Several wise men whose opinions no one sought warned that the risk of total annihilation prevents each side from preemptively attacking the other, thus justifying the proliferation — just in case — of weapons of mass destruction. They called it Mutually Assured Destruction, MAD for short. Other wise men retorted, with no less pathos, that hatred and greed are energies that cannot be compressed indefinitely, and that they must be vented from time to time, thus rendering war a natural if somewhat inelegant necessity, like farting.

No one protested. Not a single voice rose against the demagogues who preach and profit from war. No one dared to send to hell the politicians who incite it, the economists who justify it, the financiers who invest in it, and the generals who send their troops to battle, while the rest of us, imbeciles that we are, are forced to wield the sword and die. Even the professional dissenters, ill-informed and opinionated, kept quiet, their meek intellect anesthetized, their vocal cords numbed by fear. It was as if a collective apathy, a malignant aphasia had forever stifled common sense.

♦

Torn by decades of civil strife, corruption, inept governance, and poverty, several nations fell like gangrenous limbs in an orgy of blood-letting that turned rivers red and fields into open graves. Unable to trade with now impoverished client-states, and spurned by their former political and business partners, industrialized nations collapsed under the weight of their own economic gigantism. Fanatically self-absorbed, itching for a fight, they restarted old sectarian conflicts they no longer understood but did not have the courage to stop.

The end came a little after eight, on a dusky, moonless night when two laser-guided projectile exploded and ignited the sky 10,000 meters above Earth. The heavens parted. An eerie, blinding, all-consuming glow turned the sky blood-red. Electromagnetic pulses set off a massive chain reaction that silenced all communication satellites and knocked out power from pole to pole, from zenith to nadir, from first meridian east to first meridian west. The conflagration released direct ionizing and thermal radiation in the infrared and ultraviolet spectra and unleashed hurricane-force winds. The thermal pulse kindled firestorms that coalesced into a mass inferno. The high overpressure and cyclonic airstreams that accompanied the blast upsurge collapsed buildings, trapping people and exposing them to flying debris in a radius of 300 miles. Ruptured gas lines, spilt fuels, and electrical short circuits widened the fires kindled by thermal radiation. The initial fireball lofted radioactive dust and ash into the thermosphere, causing deadly lightning-induced electron precipitation. The residue floated back to earth in a matter of days. An estimated 42 million men, women and children died in the aftermath.

Others lost their hair. Their teeth fell out. Their gums dissolved. Blood oozed from the corners of their eyes. They felt no pain, they said, just an overpowering, unrelenting fatigue. These are "premonitory symptoms," declared the Federal Emergency Management Agency. The language of disaster is so laconic, so antiseptically vague. Neutron and gamma rays work slowly. But they kill in the end.

Episodic at first, famines spread like wildfire. Infant mortality was high and widespread. There were other casualties: What little food could be scraped to keep the heart pumping proved to be less than enough for the gray matter. Nearly a billion people suffered irreversible brain damage. Asylums were full. More were desperately needed to contain a swelling tide of insanity, but none was built, and the overflow spilled into the streets, along with the homeless, the sick, the dead, and the dying. For some absurd reason, men 17 to 59 were in uniform, training for the front or patrolling the streets. Everyone was armed. Looting spread during the long, searing summer, and thousands died at the hands of vigilantes, mercenaries, or roaming bands of thugs, all dispensing their own brand of justice.

A great stillness visited upon the realm. Survivors embraced and shed tears of shame and atonement, and they spoke of turning swords into plowshares. And a thousand score and ten passed. But lo and behold, the women ceased to bear fruit and the men became ill with madness and took daggers to their own hearts to smite the evil that festered within. And from the fertile plains of Ukraine to the icy peaks of the Antarctic plateau, from the distant shores of Easter Island to Bhutan's ethereal summits, there was not a voice, not a murmur, not a thistle, not a single blade of grass. Instead, emptiness reigned, vast, final. Time has stood still.

◆

Those who claimed that *"the end of the world"* isn't what it used to be, that a *"nuclear winter that would usher a life-extinguishing arctic night"* is a myth that was laid to rest [like global warming] in the potter's field of doomsday predictions, are regurgitating their words, along with their rotting viscera.

I can still hear the hysterical recitations of half-crazed preachers who gloat at the calamities they'd been longing for:

"All ye blasphemers shall be hanged by the tongue until it cleaves and forks like that of a snake. Women who adorn themselves for the purpose of adultery shall be suspended by the hair over a pool of boiling magma. The men who knew them shall be hung by their testicles and their heads lowered slowly into the pool of lava. Doubters and nonbelievers shall be cast in a pit of creeping things that will torment them. Men who take on the role of women in a sexual way and women who take on the role of men shall be dragged up a great cliff by angry angels and hurled to the bottom. They will then be forced up it, over and over again, ceaselessly, to their doom. Women who had life ripped out of their bellies shall be thrust up to their necks in a lake formed from the blood and gore that issued from their loins. They shall forever be tormented by the spirits of their unborn children. And those who performed the abortions shall spend eternity wading in a mire of foul matter and blood...."

◆

To ease the despair that incongruities evoke, I summon my third eye and weave another lucid dream of excruciating clarity through which momentous events are replayed and preserved:

128

My father's arrest by the French Gestapo; I was three; the execution of ten old men in a French hamlet by baby-faced German soldiers. I was five. I saw them crumple, lifeless, on the cobbled sidewalk. I remember staring at the pitiful mass of inert, scrunched, lifeless bodies, blood oozing from their mouths and noses, their lifeless eyes staring in the void like the eyes of a doll. It began to rain. The downpour washed away the blood as onlookers scattered and dissolved in a gray, sulfur-laden mist. I also remember telling myself over and over that I'd been treated to a grotesque spectacle, a dramatization of unimaginable realism, mere cinema noir. I remembered the deadly saturation bombing of Bucharest by U.S. forces and the atrocities committed by invading Russian forces in Romania. I remembered a gray, smoke-shrouded, sooty Manhattan skyline as I stood in mute stupefaction on the deck of the SS Constitution. I remembered the assassination of John F. Kennedy, of his brother Robert, of Malcom X and Martin Luther King. I relived the gruesome spectacle of the collapsing Twin Towers on 9/11, 2001. Yet another carnage in a school in the United States, this time in Uvalde, Texas, the immense distress of families, a serious speech by the president, then nothing, until the next. Americans have known this desperate cycle by heart since the Sandy Hook massacre in 2012. That of Parkland, in 2018, had not changed anything despite the exceptional mobilization of students who had escaped. The latter had thought it possible to bring a country sick of its violence to reason and its elected representatives to their responsibilities, but they had failed. If there is still an American exceptionalism, it is to tolerate that schools are regularly transformed into blood-stained shooting ranges. Indeed, Americans are killing each other, and the Republican Party is looking elsewhere, complicit by ideology in the tragedies that follow. Decades of skull-stuffing have meant that its elected officials no longer even need the rule of the main gun lobby, the National Rifle Association, crippled by crises, to oppose any legislation governing this particularly juicy market. The defense of the Second Amendment relating to the right to bear arms, understood in its most absolutist sense, has become an almost sacred duty that now escapes any probe and review. The families of the victims must be content with the vacant expression and sham *"thoughts"* and *"prayers"* of their representatives. There were more than 20,000 firearm deaths in 2021. There were 200 mass shootings in the United States in the first 145 days of 2022. These monstrosities date back to 1949 and have only multiplied.

The leaders claim that the country suffers from a "mental health problem." This is a despicable lie repeated by ultra-right politicians to curry favor with their base—all revolver, rifle, machine gun fanatics. The U.S. counts 322 million inhabitants ... and more than 400 million firearms.

◆

In his satirical essay, *The Decline and Fall of Practically Everybody*, the American writer and literary critic, Will Cuppy (1884-1949) peels off the deeds and gestures of the great of this world. From the summits of Egypt's pharaonic pyramids and their pre-Columbian counterparts to ancient Greece, from Antiquity to our modern era, from Europe's absolute monarchs to Russia's tsars, all the oddities and turpitudes that characterize humankind are placed under the unerring scrutiny of the author's magnifying glass.

Rendered with acerbic wit, Cuppy's commentaries remind us that, sooner or later, empires stagger, imperceptibly at first, and then collapse in a deafening din. During the last two decades, America has been in a tailspin. The pandemic has revealed its weaknesses, exposed and exacerbated—for those who still believed in Santa Claus—the realization of a colossus weakened by serious political, social, economic, and cultural problems. The nation's infrastructures are in a state of putrefaction. The middle class is in ruins; the rich are getting richer. A hedonistic mindset, "I want it all and I want it now," prevent Americans from taking things seriously. The public education system, utilitarian at best, encourages neither erudition nor critical thinking. A climate of ferocious anti-intellectualism, nascent neo-fascism, and a personality trait that predisposes Americans to believe that they are entitled to privileges that *others* do not deserve — all this has contributed to the enfeeblement of a country that, not long ago, was still the envy of the world. If we can draw a lesson from the current crisis, it would be to make the post-mortem of a political system that favors the privileged classes, while inequality, inertia, egotism, and a profit motive that undervalues human life and overrates the commodities that sustain continue to obscure the obscenity of exceptionalism. Certainly, the advent of the coronavirus is an alarming crisis, but the same is true with a political culture that has produced a virulent presidency and a climate that continues to infect and weaken what is left of democracy. The most optimistic among us say that everything is still going quite well compared to what awaits us. The helm is broken, and the ship of state ship is adrift.

I rarely know where I'm headed. I often get lost. But the urge to find my way out of the follies to which I'm being treated is so compelling that I keep dreaming. The journey is tedious at times and many an image once indelibly etched in my mind shrivels up and dies a thousand deaths as I uncap my pen. Then night returns to deliver me from day and I reenter the dream. I may be dreaming even as I tell you this, my third eye now in ever sharper focus. Catch me if you can. It's all a shell game.

> *"Life can only be understood backwards;*
> *but it must be lived forwards."*
> **— Søren Kierkegaard (1813-1855)**

ACKNOWLEDGEMENTS—I am indebted to my parents, learned, urbane, fair-minded, for instilling a love of books and an appreciation for music, art, and philosophy, for sparing me the enslavement of religious indoctrination, and for enduring, if not always endorsing, my wildest antics. To my mother, a selfless, unassuming, cultured woman of great refinement, I owe my admiration for the beauty and symmetry of nature, and my love of animals. From my father, a loving, iron-willed and incorruptible man who abhorred ostentation and pretense, I learned that self-esteem and a reverence for truth confer infinitely greater gifts than money or material comfort.

I salute my teachers, those I pleased when I applied myself and those I exasperated when I didn't. Their erudition, pedagogical skills, and saintly patience for the lazy, unfocused, mercurial, and rebellious student I was helped lay the foundations on which I would erect a lifetime career of endless beginnings.

I can never sufficiently acknowledge the immense influence several writers, poets, and philosophers had on the constantly evolving person I would become and, by extension, on the ideas I would champion. Their prose, verses, insights, and eye-opening reflections resonate as intensely today as they did in the days of my youth. Most were French. One was denied a Christian funeral for penning vitriolic anti-clerical tracts. Four were imprisoned, the first for denouncing the bestiality of colonialism; the second—the son of a prostitute—for "vagabondage, lewd acts, and other offenses against public decency;" the third for stretching the limits of literary freedom in pamphlets that mixed raw eroticism with civil disobedience. The fourth spoke for the common man and rose with uncommon bravery against the corruption of the clergy and the decadence of the military establishment.

Three were Russian. One of them, a novelist, essayist, and journalist, explored human psychology in the social, political, and spiritual milieu of his time. His works are populated by neurotics and lunatics, the kind who become pope, king, dictator, tyrant, president. It took as deranged a genius like him to understand and paint the frailties, aberrations, and horrors of life. Reading him is like descending into a snake pit of insanity. The poor man had epilepsy. He was sentenced to death for writing anti-tsarist tracts (the sentence was commuted at the last moment). He spent four years in a Siberian prison camp, followed by six years of compulsory military service in exile — enough to madden anyone. The second, a ruthless satirist, imparts surrealism and the grotesque with an unusual aura of normality. The third, the one that shocked me to my core, was a *"professional revolutionary,"* and theorist of anarchism influenced by Hegelian thought. The man was a closet authoritarian who condoned violence, and an odious anti-Semite. I did agree with him when he remarked, *"Everything will pass, and the world will perish but [Beethoven's] Ninth Symphony will endure forever."*

My other mentors wrote in Arabic, English, Dutch, German, Sanskrit, and Spanish. Three hailed from Ireland; one did not survive the spurious puritanism of his Victorian milieu. One died insane — as do those who seek shelter from the battering storm of reality in the sanctuary of delirium. The third was excommunicated for trying to resolve the conflict between religious dogma and secular knowledge, and for departing from Aristotelian thought by emphasizing the depth of human ignorance. All were free thinkers, rebels, defenders of secularism, all long-deceased but whose heterodoxy and reformist ideas still inspire new generations of resisters, heroes, and martyrs. All were iconoclasts, now long dead, but whose works and the reformist ideas they conveyed still inspire new generations of mavericks-in-training.

It is with equal reverence that I thank my friends, few as they are, attentive and loyal, whose encouragement helped immensely during difficult moments of illness, introspection, and self-criticism during the gestation of this work.

I must also salute some readers, especially social media busybodies who snap at any concept they don't understand or that contradicts their ingrained beliefs while draping themselves in anonymity. The vitriol, acrid diatribes, and ad-hominem attacks that my writings inspire is ambrosia to my ears. It reinforces my conviction that in this era of lies and unreason all opinions have equal weight but that only the truth, rare and easily distorted, unnerving, and often cruel, must prevail. Sadly, the evanescent nature of history's impact on succeeding generations does not include a built-in sense of anticipation for the horrors to come. Whereas fiction can take liberties with the future, it cannot, must not, revise, embellish, add to, or disfigure the past—as is the annoying habit of "historical novels." Nor can journalism alter the present. Fiction may use metaphor and allegory to tell inconvenient truths. Journalism must not fabricate facts. To be credible, journalism can't afford to be harmless.

◆
◆ ◆

Born in Paris, **W. E. Gutman** is a retired Franco-American journalist and published author. The former international editor of the late-great futurist magazine, *OMNI*, and the co-founder of a defense publication monitoring the proliferation of weapons of mass destruction, he was U.S. editor of a Moscow-based science journal. He later served as a press officer at Israel's Consulate General in New York. He reported from Central America from 1994 to 2006.

www.ingramcontent.com/pod-product-compliance
Lightning Source LLC
Chambersburg PA
CBHW031210270326
41931CB00006B/503